Courting Triumph

Courting Triumph

by

Virginia Wade

with Mary Lou Mellace

MAYFLOWER BOOKS, INC.,
575 LEXINGTON AVENUE,
NEW YORK CITY 10022.

ISBN 0-8317-1800-5

FIRST AMERICAN EDITION

To A.L. and P.W.

We would like to thank E. for assistance
in typing the manuscript.

Black-and-white illustrations

Colour illustrations

ACKNOWLEDGMENTS

BLACK-AND-WHITE ILLUSTRATIONS
[1]A. & M. Cole, Le-Roye Productions
[2]Sport and General
[3]Barratts Photo Press
[4]Alex C. Cowper
[5]Associated Press
[6]*The Times*
[7]New York "Apples"
[8]Robert D. Brient, Texas
[9]Press Association
[10]London Express

COLOUR ILLUSTRATIONS
[1]Art Seitz
[2]Barry Rabinowitz
[3]A. & M. Cole, Le-Roye Productions

"Ah, my beloved, fill the cup that clears
Today of past regrets and future fears."

Edward Fitzgerald: *The Rubáiyát of Omar Khayyám*

Courting Triumph

Wimbledon

I've been here sixteen years in a row and have never managed to catch sight of it. Now barring anything short of divine intervention, it's straight ahead. The long-sought-after light at the end of a sixteen-year-old tunnel.

I've played this tournament for exactly half of my life.

I'm in the final for the first time.

The Queen is watching. Everybody is watching.

I'm going to win this thing if I have to kill myself to do it.

I am going home today with something I have dreamed about from the moment I knew it existed. And I'm going to send everybody else home with a piece of it.

Not one of these people will get out of this place unaffected.

This is not a mass of unidentifiable humanity. I know each one here and each one watching on the television, listening on the radio.

They've all been invited to this private party and they won't leave without a memento of the occasion.

We are all co-producers of this event, every last one of us.

And when I've won this title I will look in the eyes of every single face and say thank you.

Thank you for believing in me.

Thank you for caring.

Thank you for waiting.

I hope you are all happy. You have made me very happy.

The first point against Betty Stove in the final of Wimbledon, I lost. To be more accurate, Betty won it.

A few polite people clapped. Those were the brave ones. The rest just pretended it hadn't happened.

I'd played a careful first serve, cautiously stayed on the baseline, was forced to come into the net and watched a lob over my left shoulder land well in.

It amused me to think of the impact the first point in a match like this has on people; as if it symbolises everything that will follow. They chatter away during the warm-up, but when the umpire says "Ready, play" everyone, but everyone watches that first point.

I was glad it was over.

The beginning of a match is important, but I knew that today, all things considered, the opening points would be nothing more than exposition before the thick of the real plot.

Today was different.

It was the centenary year of the tournament, the Queen's Jubilee; she had come to watch and it was my first time in a Wimbledon final.

I served again; medium paced to Betty's forehand. She returned it, I hit a forehand, not very well, and she missed it. 15 all.

Now there was vigorous applause. The English have a reputation (not without justification) for fairness and impartiality. Today they felt more than a decent excuse to be relieved of such obligation. No token show of neutrality; they were happy to be able to clap, even if it was for Betty's error.

My main objective in this opening game was to get all my mechanical faculties working. By habit I took deep breaths, making sure I walked with measured pace, dropping my shoulders to relax. Legs can turn to lead. I ran down every ball to counteract the possibility.

Betty would hit some uninhibited shots. That wasn't my aim. I just wanted to be satisfied that my modest objectives were being met.

That was another difference. One of the prime reasons I was here in the final this year was because I had objectives.

At 40–30 to me, Betty played two audacious points. She had an advantage, but I came back with a winning first serve. It's always a good sign if you can bring out your best serves in the crunch.

After three more deuces I won the game, and the crowd leapt at the opportunity to show its approval. The game had taken five minutes.

I walked to the umpire's stand and sat, relieved. It was the biggest match of my life, but then I didn't want to think about that.

My throat was dry. I had some water and went through the usual routine of towelling off, putting cold water on my forehead to make me as alert as possible. It was quite cool out there; one of those breezy days when the clouds are so low the sun never breaks through for long.

"It wasn't a great game, but you won it. Leave it behind. Keep thinking forward. You'll get into it soon."

I was still slightly stunned by the occasion. I mean, "My God, all I have to do is win one more match." My mind was under tight rein. There was no rope for any disorderly thoughts. "Don't think about anything. Watch the ball. Hit it back in court no matter what. Don't think what happens if your body freezes up on you."

My matches during this tournament had all been purposeful and deliberate. I was calm but at the same time totally alert. The opening round against Jo Durie got just as much attention as the semifinal round against Chris Evert. And why shouldn't it have? Without a win in the first round there is no semifinal. The last thing I wanted to do was break the circuit of the stability responsible for getting me here.

Earlier in the day I'd sat alone for twenty minutes in the members' stand on the Centre Court before I went in to change, before they even had the net up. The court looked bigger, the light and darker shades of green mown stripes, unerringly straight, the lines freshly coated with white chalk. It had been flawlessly manicured for its climactic day.

In the corner the band of the Welsh Guards arrived, resplendent in uniforms of scarlet. They discreetly assembled their music stands, tuned up and began a medley from Rodgers and Hammerstein.

People were filtering into the stands. Already in the standing-room area they'd made themselves comfortable, taking their last opportunity of sitting before their time of vigil came. They'd been there since noon. Some had been lining up outside the grounds for hours. There were those who had even slept there overnight.

I didn't want them to see me. I liked being anonymous, one of them. Besides I was here to think, to orient myself; it was the Centre Court I'd been on dozens of times and no one of them. Besides, I was here to think, to orient myself; it when I came out to play at two o'clock I wouldn't have time to gaze around and absorb the details.

Sure I knew the Centre Court, maybe better than any other court in the world. I can tell you what time it is when the sun's shadow crosses diagonally over the service line. I can tell you what sort of numerals are on that unequivocal clock at the south end. I can tell you the wind velocity by the way the linen awning flaps above the Royal Box. I can even tell you if a new pigeon has joined the group which

23

roost up in the ceiling above the stands. I can tell you all that. But that's academic.

What I needed to know now was what would happen to me when I walked out there on the threshold of an irretrievable moment.

I absorbed it. I created the illusion of the packed stands; the colours; the noise; the mood. I started to react to it. I stepped outside myself and became a member of the crowd watching me play some points. Then I played them from inside my viewpoint with the fifteen thousand fans surrounding me.

I knew I was ready. I could look back on the old days with defiant detachment. Those fifteen years when games had cascaded by and at times I'd changed ends in a daze of confusion, the Royal Box my only clue which end was which. I had reached the quarterfinals only once in ten years from 1962 to 1971. The middle Saturday of the tournament was my biggest hurdle. To be in the second week was a target I hardly hit. I seemed always to be spending that Saturday at the champagne party drowning my sorrows.

The romanticism of youthful success had got me into those messes. In my early days I did not want to be an "experienced" player or a "veteran winner". Experience meant drudgery. It might even mar the lustre of my "spontaneity", a depressing possibility. My whole performance was based on the concept of improvisation.

I wanted to play matches without having to think about them. To extemporise, as it were, like the musical geniuses who sat at the keyboard and created, in a parlour full of awestruck admirers. If I saw an older player finally win I felt terribly sympathetic. How could she have had the patience to wait so long? Now at least she could retire (I never considered whether she wanted to), not having made that last gasp in vain.

With classic irony, little did I suspect that it would take sixteen tries for me to get to the finals and that Betty and I would be the oldest finalists since 1913 when Dorothea Chambers at the age of thirty-five beat Mrs R. J. Mcnair, aged thirty-six.

Transient memories of the fifteen failures left me unmoved with the fortification of security. No one thought I could win any more; the public thought I was past it. The press had overestimated me too soon; now they underestimated me.

But I was invulnerable. I'd said all along that if I got to the final of Wimbledon this year I'd win. The answer someone gave me was, "Then make sure you get to the final."

The atmosphere was expectant, festive, and I was at the centre of it. If there was an afternoon designed perfectly to meet all specifications this was it.

I was going to make it mine.

I suppose the players on the tour have their own particular reasons for calling me "Wild Woman".

When Rosie Casals introduced it for the first time in Australia in 1968 I assumed it was because of my flare-ups on the court.

They stopped using it for a while, but since my hair has been cut they're back to using it again. Actually I don't mind it at all. I think it's a rather appropriate name.

To them it was probably because of my outward shows of temper on the court. To me it's something basic and indigenous to my character.

I'm one of those people whose brain and body react inseparably. In other words, almost as with an animal, instinct is my strongest form of guidance. With me the genesis of any reaction is below the conscious level in the instinctive sphere.

It's something I never realised till one afternoon this spring when it suddenly dawned on me. I was practising at Madison Square Garden for a Team Tennis match. The circus was also in town at the Garden. I wanted to go but our playing schedule conflicted with their performances. So during a break in practice I went back behind the arena to at least have a look at the animals in the menagerie.

It was almost as good as a zoo. Better in some ways because there were a few off-duty clowns sleeping undisturbed by the litany of the huge family of animals; trumpeting elephants, neighing horses, screeching monkeys.

I stopped to stroke the nose of a piebald pony and

chatted to a few of the friendly dogs. But in the end it was the wild cats with their irresistible power that drew me back for a second look.

While I stood about three feet from his cage, one magnificent leopard paced ceaselessly in a space of about five by eight feet. He walked the length of the cage, pivoted and headed directly for the opposite end only to start all over again.

I stood and watched him the way one sometimes watches ocean waves roll in and out, absolutely magnetised by the movement and unable to avert my eyes. I was hooked by this totally instinctive animal and the unmistakably physical terms in which he reacted to his environment.

All at once it clicked. I suddenly recognised the same tendency in myself. This was an animal whose mind and body were unified in every sense of the word. As with the leopard, all my perceptions, mental and emotional, want to be translated physically. Certainly as a child, before reason could colour my actions, boundless energy and physical expression made me what the players on the tour would surely have called "Wild Child".

All I wanted was to run around outside. If it wasn't spending hours diving in and out of the sea it was doing acrobatics on the lawn. If it wasn't hide-and-seek or climbing trees around the neighbourhood then it was polevaulting in the garden.

I wasn't exactly a ragamuffin but my black mop of

curls with a will of its own sat sometimes bundled up on top to keep from falling over my blue eyes. If eyes can look both innocent and devilish, mine did, mirroring one or the other of my most frequent moods. With a long back and bandy legs my body had a lean look. almost like a playful foal. I ran almost before I walked.

Little girls' games were sweet and more aesthetically attractive than the vigorous athletic ones, but they couldn't keep me involved for any length of time. Somehow there was more urgency to play the active games. Quiet ones would always wait.

There was an article in a Durban paper right after I won Wimbledon. My favourite neighbour there in South Africa remembers me doing cartwheels in her flat overlooking our house. "Can you do this, Mrs Walker?" I asked, while anxious glances were cast at the glass door to the balcony. Apparently I kept Mrs Walker's attention. "I spent most of the time counting while Virginia saw how long she could stand on her head . . . From my window I could see her prancing around their garden doing all sorts of acrobatics."

Even though it was indoors it was a treat visiting Mrs Walker. I thought living in a block of flats must be exciting. We had always lived in large and rambling vicarages, my father being a clergyman. First in Bournemouth, where I was born and stayed for eleven months. Then Cape Town for four years, and eventually Durban where we settled.

Vicarages all seem to have certain features in

common; such as ludicrous architectural plans, neither efficient nor convenient. In Cape Town the house had been spread out in the most disorganised fashion. In Durban the house was slightly less rambling but almost as impractical in its layout. Another common feature is their immense gardens. Ours in Durban, however, scarcely matched the traditional image of the vicarage lawn where tea was served on Sunday afternoons. There was a small cultivated section for show. Just out of obvious sight was the rest of it, uncultivated, which with a little imagination could have been the very jungle itself.

This was where I spent most of my time. There was too big a difference in age for my brothers (Anthony, ten years older than I, and Christopher, eight years older) to really care for my games. My sister, Judy, two years older, was more the quiet, cutting-out-paper-dolls type. So, I usually played with other children from the neighbourhood.

When I'd exhausted all their collective energies I would continue on my own. Preferably in the garden near enough to the kitchen so that I could race in and out to share my exploits with my mother. She was always around. Mostly all her time was taken up organising the family; cooking for us, washing, looking after us. Though the schedule revolved around Daddy and his work, she was the centre of all our lives. Born in Grahamstown, of a Scottish father and an English mother, her family had returned to

England for a holiday when the First World War broke out. Being stranded as a child during those bleak war years left her with a disinclination towards living there permanently. They went back to South Africa at the first available opportunity.

However, when she returned to England as a postgraduate at Cambridge, she fell in love with my father, then Chaplain of Downing College. Although she had sworn never to marry an Englishman, four years later she gave up her maths teaching in South Africa to go back to England and they were married in 1934.

A few years later they went to Paris where Daddy had been appointed Chaplain of the British Embassy Church. For three years they lived there, by which time the war clouds were darkening. As the Germans were closing in on Paris, they were evacuated along with the masses of refugees and managed to return to England on literally the last boat that left from St. Malo. It was ten days after the Dunkirk débâcle.

Daddy became Vicar of Holy Trinity Church, Bournemouth and a Chaplain to the Forces. In 1946 we left England when he was requested to accept an important parish in Cape Town.

Daddy was constantly busy at the church as Vicar of St Paul's, Archdeacon of Durban. He really had a seven-day-a-week job and certainly more than a nine-to-five day. If anyone had a problem and needed him, he was on call to go to their assistance at any time.

Dinner was the focal point for the family. It was the only time of day when everyone would be together. It was hard to get a word in amongst the endless overlapping conversations, arguments or laughter, but I don't think anyone got left out. There would be the inevitable telephone interruptions for Daddy. Being the fastest to the 'phone, I became an excellent secretary.

We four children were expected to be punctual for meals, fulfil our allocated chores, complete our respective homework. Mostly everything revolved around home with its definite disciplinary boundaries. Providing we stayed within bounds and met our responsibilities, we were free to do whatever we wanted.

My choice was to be outside in the garden, up a tree, or seeing how far I could walk on my hands.

There were trips I especially clamoured for. A treat for me was swimming at the beach with my father or watching the ships come in while he'd prepare his sermons. We'd go down by the entrance to the harbour in Durban to see the freighters, tankers or passenger ships. I knew which company each ship belonged to; whether they were coming from Southampton, Cape Town or Australia, and I'd wave furiously to the little specks of sailors lining the decks.

If we were really lucky we might be there when the whalers returned with their catch. I'd no conception of quite how large whales could be. Huge ships flanked by a whale on either side were dwarfed by their magnitude. I knew nothing of their frailty as a species at the hands of humans. It seemed so awesome that these enormous creatures had been killed at all, let alone by one small harpoon.

I was so energetic I don't know how Daddy managed to keep me quiet long enough to concentrate on his sermons. To begin with, I didn't understand very much about what he was doing, but later on, seeing him in his cassocks and gowns preaching in front of all the people, I would imitate the attentive faces of the congregation and try not to wriggle.

I always enjoyed church. Even when I was too young to understand the proper meaning, the grandeur and reverence attracted me. We went several times on Sundays when Daddy was officiating or preaching, but never was religion forced down our throats. Except for Grace at meals and of course prayers before going to sleep, I don't remember any incidents of "indoctrination".

Till I was seven, apart from the occasional outing, home life was the centre of my world. There was always plenty of family around, but I found most of my entertainment outside. Probably because I had to wait till my seventh birthday to attend, I loved school. My mother had unorthodox theories on education. She taught all four of us at home until we were seven, before allowing us to be exposed to the establishment methods of education.

I think she felt she could do as professional a job

herself as she had been a teacher at one stage. Also she was sure we would develop more original thought processes. She was always insistent throughout my school life that I should be an individual. I didn't have to do something just because everyone else did.

When I was finally old enough to go, I felt as if I'd reached a great stage in my maturity. I'd had fun at home till Judy had gone to school herself two years earlier. Since then it had become more and more dull.

I liked the lessons. Right away I developed a bent for the more exact subjects which one was able to work out. I liked getting accurate answers in arithmetic, grammar, spelling and reading. I didn't lean so comfortably towards history or geography. They sounded interesting, but there didn't seem to be any logic. I thought I should love history. The stories were fascinating, but what was the point in all those crazy dates if there could never be a definite answer? No matter how much effort I put into it, I never flowed with it the way I did with the more black and white subjects. Nevertheless, I came top of my class and was pushed up a year.

That flair for exactitude is probably why tennis is so much more suited to me than a less precise sport. Tennis is definite. You either hit a ball in or out. You either win or lose. There's nothing ambiguous about it.

From the start I was one of the school leaders in athletic endeavours. I'd be the one who picked her team for the daily sporting combats, trying with all my might to attain not only a team win but an individual record. I can still see so clearly in my mind that field at the bottom of the school grounds at Gordon Road Girls' School where we'd pursue our schoolgirl games with such seriousness and pride.

Despite my total preoccupation with games (before school, during break, after school) netball, rounders, and running weren't enough. They finally became dull, both at home and at school. I'd exhausted every variation I could think of.

I was ready for something more.

1–0 Wade.

The minute was up. I walked back to the baseline.

"You have to expect anything . . . this isn't Chris Evert or Margaret Court." They would get deep solid first serves in and I could start immediately to get my timing. That's what I wanted to do those next few games, but Betty could just as easily serve a double as an ace.

Her first serve was a fault. I moved in slightly for the second serve. "It's normally as hard as her first . . . I can't really press." A double. 0–15. The second point her serve bounced up rather high. I returned it and she jabbed a comparatively easy forehand volley into the net. Almost the same thing happened on the next point.

34

The court seemed much harder than it had two days ago when I played Chris. It had been sunny. Each day the court was rolled and played on, it got firmer and faster.

0−40. Her toss was over to the left a little and just when I thought she was going to catch it and start over again, she pounded it in. My backhand return was sloppy, into the top of the net. "You fell backwards on that . . . keep your wrist firm . . . go out and meet the ball."

Ha ha. The next ball I couldn't even touch. An ace. I smiled. A longish tentative rally. Deuce. Her advantage. Her game.

"Oh, that's ridiculous . . . that was your own fault . . . if you have 40−0 you win the next point." I did not want anyone in the arena to have a chance, even for a minute, to start in with that "Old Virginia" bit.

Tennis needs the media. We tennis players depend on the press for publicity, but, by the same token, they wouldn't have a job if it weren't for us. So there is an agreement of mutual interdependence and respect between both sides.

Over the years I have appreciated their support, companionship and knowledge on a personal level. However, a few of them are more concerned with professional motives than the unspoken inviolable terms of a friendship. A Virginia Wade story becomes a commodity evaluated purely for saleability with no respect to private feelings.

At times I've been totally fed up by the way these particular journalists kept trying to jockey me into the cliché characterisation of the tennis court termagant. Whether I

35

won or lost, my "temper" was at the bottom of it.

I objected to the use of the preconceived image which does so little to develop and so much to impede progress. When they watched me play they unobjectively ignored the present and in Mantra-like repetition recalled the past. They had not written about me hundreds of times; they had written once and repeated it hundreds of times.

The point is that while it is easier simply to categorise and be done with it, it is not always strictly accurate.

Imperceptible changes are taking place. It happens.

Life is not a static thing. Whether or not that is convenient for certain members of the press, I don't know. But no one wishes to have his inevitable evolution refused credence.

I am no exception.

At nine years old I never kept shoes on. They were anathema to me. The moment I came home from school I kicked them off. My soles must have been as hard then from running around outside as they are now from all the running on court.

The floors in the old Durban houses were often made of stone as a relief from the subtropical heat. This particular afternoon my feet were bare as usual. I could feel the coolness on them as I stood by the open cupboard and examined the object in my hand. The lack of interest I was experiencing in my usual games had brought me in early and I was lost for something to do.

My mother never tolerated complaints of boredom. She responded to my grumbles that afternoon by issuing the task of clearing up the junk cupboard. Here I was rummaging disinterestedly through discarded raincoats, umbrellas, deflated footballs, single shoes, piles of old *Country Life*; the usual debris of a large family.

I was about to add this object to the tidy pile when a spark of curiousity arrested me. I'd seen tennis racquets before. My reaction had always been indifferent. They were pieces of sports equipment. But this one in my hand registered possibilities.

I examined it. "It must be quite old," I thought. "I wonder whose it was. Daddy never played tennis. It can't be his. Nor did Mummy. Anthony plays, but he has his in a press safely out of reach. Perhaps it got stranded at the vicarage after a church bazaar." There were always some odd objects left around after one of my father's church bazaars.

I cradled it. "It's so heavy it must have belonged to a big strong man," I guessed. "I'll have to hold it with two hands." I had an instant image of myself hitting balls against our vicarage wall.

In my usual fashion I forgot about cleaning the cupboard and raced outside to try it.

"I'll use the front wall of the house. The drive's a bit bumpy, but it doesn't matter." I tried to wrap my small fingers around the handle. Bigger hands than mine had turned the grip shiny and dark from use. I smelled my palm, unmistakably perfumed by the leather. It was so heavy I couldn't hold it by the handle so I choked up on the throat.

"This is how they do it. Bounce the ball, swing at it with the racquet." It bounced off the wall and flew by me before I could recover from the realisation that I had hit my first tennis ball. I tried again. Bounce, hit, thud. Bounce, hit, thud. Bounce, ooops. The gravel driveway made for some pretty funny bounces.

I took another look at it. It was pretty clever the way all the strings were woven through one another without any mistakes. In fact, I liked the look altogether of this old racquet whose paint and varnish were slightly yellowed.

This was more than just one of my ten-minute enthusiasms. I stayed out there and played until my mother called me for dinner. My arm was sore from the weight of the racquet.

It had long been too dark to see the ball, but I didn't want to stop. Here was a game that would finally make real demands on my boundless energy. I got to run *and* hit a ball besides. I loved the quick and visible results when the ball and racquet connected and I was tantalised by the idea that there was something very exact about it.

This racquet gave me a tremendous sense of ownership and purpose; buried under the pile of junk a family of six can accumulate, it had been meant for me to find and make my own.

I didn't entertain any long-range visions of being a professional tennis player, but that night as I ate dinner my new acquisition leaned against my chair. I peeked occasional glances at it and thought only of when I could play next.

At one all, I played a perfect game.

There's a theory that the best time to break a player with a dominating serve is in the first game while they're probably not quite warmed up. It had succeeded against me often enough. Then it became a main goal not to drop my opening serve. I'd win it, take my second serve less seriously and lose that.

Today I was aware of everything. I won my second service game to love. I tossed the ball in my left hand back confidently. It wasn't required for a second serve.

Most of the players have acquired the habit of using only one ball to serve with. If it's a fault they simply turn round and ask a hopefully alert ballboy for another. My habit of holding two has never left me. It seems an unnecessary interruption to be searching for a ball before a second serve, and I don't need the use of my left hand for any two-handed shots.

My Team Tennis teammates tell me that whenever I'm a trifle flustered on court I chuck the remaining ball out of my hand into the backstop and request two more.

These habits that players have are fascinating. Betty's always walking backwards when a ballboy throws her the ball. She won't tread on the lines of the court between points. I can't imagine how that compulsion arose or what it's protection from; she must have both won and lost matches while avoiding lines. Bjorn Borg, on the other hand, doesn't shave during a tournament, which is why, during Wimbledon, he always sports a beard.

My stride was buoyant. The crowd was relaxing a bit. If there is a rapport between you, they project your feelings onto themselves. Whatever their collective vision notices, soon comes back in atmospheric waves. I've learned to cope with that. They were convinced now that whatever happened I would be in control. They could trust me.

Amidst applause I walked to the Royal Box end. There's always a temptation to glance up there, especially today. One doesn't often have the opportunity of examining the Queen at such close proximity. When we'd turned to curtsy to her on the way in, I was chuffed that she was wearing almost the identical shade of pink as I. "Lie de vin", as Teddy Tinling calls it.

You can't help being a little self-conscious playing within such close scrutiny of the most majestic individual in

The beginnings of a sandcastle on
a Cape Town beach

"Sour grapes" judging by the
expression on 5-year-old
Virginia's face

Family portrait overlooking the esplanade at Durban.
Back row : left to right: **Christopher, Father, Virginia, Mother,**
Anthony, Toby the dog and Judy

Virginia, aged 9, in the back garden of the Vicarage in Durban

Sunday was the maid's day off

In the Durban High School Tennis Team, with best friend Liz Wiles standing on the left

With her first tennis racquet and a rare new ball

the world. *And you can't really peer straight up for a look
in case she's doing the same.*

*Perhaps I was being studied in the same way as one of her
thoroughbred horses . . . I'd consider that a compliment.*

*Some of my most respected friends compare me with a
racehorse. Instead of sending me hackneyed cards with
tennis players on, I receive reproductions of George Stubbs.*

*But I've got letters which don't altogether suggest any such
thoroughbred affiliation. "Stop putting your hair in place
when your opponent is preparing to serve. If you're worrying
about how you look you can't be concentrating on your
tennis. You stand flat-footed with your feet too wide apart.
Balance on the balls of your feet, not your heels. I recommend
a month's training with a ballet team, plus a daily diet of
Devon or Scotch beef . . ."*

I was ready ahead of Betty.

*". . . I'm glad that serve didn't go in, I was going
towards the forehand . . . be more on the point of balance
. . . you can go either way at the last moment . . . she
swats at that toss . . . you can't tell where it's going . . .
you were late on the second serve too . . . there's no time for
a backswing . . . block it back more, but early . . . hit
through the backhand . . . damn it, I'm all prepared for a
backhand return . . . she hits the line on the forehand side . . .
you did well to even scrape that back . . .*

*30–0 . . . She hasn't served wide in the right court yet
. . . be ready . . . yeah, I guessed that one . . . too bad it
was such a good serve . . . at least you're getting them back*

. . . but still late on that backhand pass . . .

40–0 . . . Give her that serve . . . it was too good . . . she can't keep serving that well . . . it's tough doing anything much when it's just bang bang like this . . . OK, come on . . ."

I walked in a little circle round the baseline, waiting for the balls to come up my end. It was up wind here. I could feel my hair being moved about.

I didn't care for that last game. There was nothing beneficial about it in any way. Not only did I not gain a single point, but I hadn't improved my judgment of the bounce.

My first serve went where I wanted it, deep in the middle. I stomped in, hit a low forehand volley which dribbled off the end of my racquet into the net. To my surprise a loud grunt of disapproval escaped me. That was the first time in the whole tournament I'd been impatient with myself. Before I served again I grabbed the ball and bounced it hard. It nearly hit me in the jaw. Definite sign of impatience.

"OK, come on . . . it doesn't matter whether you follow your serve in or not, just be decisive . . . take your time . . . be decisive . . . Great first serve . . . she can't handle that . . . keep that first serve in but keep going for it . . ."

Immediately I missed my next first serve. I rushed a bit. I didn't follow my second serve in, but hit a great forehand chip approach shot only to be caught by a lob that brought up chalk on my baseline. "Come on, Betty, where did that come from . . .?"

Another first serve miss, but I hit a perfect slice backhand

42

which stayed down low. 30–30. Again my first serve missed by a fraction. "Where's your blessed first serve . . .? Relax on it . . . remember what Ham said . . . 'take a deep breath, relax your shoulders before you serve, get your toss up to the right, easy swing . . . it's programmed to go in.' " Ham Richardson, a former US Davis Cup player had instigated the readjustment of my serve months before.

"Well, you were a trifle lucky to win that point . . . she's amazing . . . she does a great return then misses an easy volley . . . no one knows where they are with her . . ."

The game went on like that. A winner, a loser from Betty and some crazy shots from me. On an advantage point for Betty I changed my mind on a forehand and missed it. "You fool . . . you let her have that point . . ."

And the game. She broke me to lead 3–2. I couldn't believe I'd lost that game, I'd gone through all that care not to lose my first two service games and now I'd lost the third.

Why is it that one minute you'd rather die than lose the point and another you literally give it away? Will power. Why does it come and go? I've practised tennis for twenty-two years; I've thought about the game for almost as long and then for a couple of minutes I allow a lapse of will and make enough silly errors to lose a game. It's ridiculous.

Just what is it about tennis that keeps me here? Isn't there something crazy about decking out in a little white costume made specially for me (which a very particular man spent hours creating) to go racing back and forth on 1,000 or so square feet of turf, hitting a furry ball over a net in the middle? Why do grown people do this? Why was I doing this? If it wasn't crazy, what was it?

Tennis was an obsession.

After my discovery, I played every single minute I wasn't obliged to do something else. If I couldn't be playing, I talked about it constantly, and at least had the feeling of being there in some way. Paradoxically, it may have been my never-ending topic of conversation, but it was also my very own personal discovery which gave me a natural sense of privacy about it. I chattered, but I never revealed the profound effect it was having on me.

I had only to finish one game to want to play again.

Before school I would hit against the wall of our vicarage, then still get to school early to spend some time on a court without having to share with too many others.

After school I stayed late to play with anyone who was around, then went home to finish up the day where it had started; facing the wall.

Before long, the white vicarage wall was wrecked with ball marks, so my father forbade me to use it any more. I went to enormous lengths to get him to remodel the garage door so that I could use that as a wall.

If there was an obstacle it didn't last very long. I always found a way to play tennis. The only thing that could prevent me was rain, and if I missed out because of bad weather I felt most deprived.

Through all this I was absolutely certain that I would be good at this sport.

That instinct, along with the immense pleasure I had in running and the actual mechanics of hitting the ball, kept me permanently consumed with the idea of perfecting what I knew was my very own speciality.

From the beginning I had an unrestrained competitiveness in tennis. With anything else I didn't mind taking a back seat. (I didn't like it, but I could take it.) With tennis I had to be best.

It wasn't just a conceit which inspired me. My personal appropriation of a sport which was played widely in South Africa was based on what I felt to be an incontestable and objective reality: I cared more about it than the others did. If devotion was any measure, then I should be the best.

I suppose one always reacts that way about people or things that one responds to with a passion. To become protective and possessive of someone or something purely because you feel your intensity gives you that privilege.

If I wondered how everyone else felt about it, my immediate comparison was Judy. She had started playing at school a little while earlier but it did not figure definitively in her life.

I hounded her all the time to play with me in the garden where we'd hit balls through knee-high weeds. She'd get bored in no time. Of course I could never have enough.

At last, I progressed to my first prized new racquet, a junior model more suited to my skinny long-legged frame. It required some real persuasion to get this. Being the fourth and youngest child I usually got all the hand-me-downs.

Both Judy and I played in the local junior tournaments. She with a calm, almost social attitude, I with a competitiveness and determination to win.

In the under-elevens I was invincible. I remember having a really big serve and thinking it would be a shame that I had to move up to an older age group and become a small fish again. In actual fact, all of us juniors who were reasonably good went practically straight from the twelve-year-old age group to open events which stood us in good stead for the transition from the junior stage.

In South Africa there was a well-developed system of tournaments for juniors to participate in. It was like Australia where they had organised competitions weekly, and where all the good players started. However, there was always the knowledge that eventually one had to go abroad to really acquire international experience. Anyone who had competed at Wimbledon whether or not they won a single game, was considered to have achieved dazzling heights.

As a twelve-year-old it never entered my mind that I might for any length of time be a "tennis player". Not only was tennis amateur (and therefore couldn't be considered as a profession unless one became a teaching pro or ran a sports shop), but it was totally disregarded by my family as a serious occupation.

My background was so orientated towards academic professional vocations. My father had given up the opportunity of following in his father's very success-ful business in order to go into the church. He graduated from Oxford and his first job was as a chaplain at Cambridge.

My mother had graduated from Rhodes University in South Africa and furthered her studies at Cambridge. Anthony was brilliant academically and had a Rhodes Scholarship to Oxford. Christopher was at university in Natal.

They all participated in sports as a recreation. Anthony excelled at squash which overtook his tennis. Christopher was the most serious athlete of all, going through the range of track events. First he was an ardent cyclist, then pole vaulter and finally he specialised in running one mile events, gradually increasing to the marathon. He only quit a few years ago after he'd won the Swedish marathon several times.

The two of us certainly have been persistent but

while he was putting in an even harder effort than I, he was also maintaining a high-powered engineering job. Never did he derive a penny nor the recognition that a successful tennis player does.

So while never approaching tennis with any thoughts of a future, I was, nevertheless, on a day-to-day basis, nurturing dreams that I imagine are like those of a child saying "I want to be a fireman"; without any base at all.

I was quite unlike Billie Jean, for example, who told me that at the age of four she stood by the sink in her kitchen and with conviction said to her mother: "Mom, I'm gonna do something great!" At eleven she decided she was going to be a professional sports player and chose tennis as the most suitable sport.

Many other blossoming professional tennis players come from tennis playing families or were taught by their parents. Tennis is so much a part of their accepted way of life that they gradually develop in and with it. They learn things at a very young age through habit and drill rather than the alternative process of personal observation. We all know how difficult it can sometimes be to make the right behavioural choice when it's left up to us. But, for instance, if a young player is drilled never to let a bad line call bother him, he'll probably save a lot of wasted arguments.

These are the players like Chris Evert, her sister Jeanne, Sandy Mayer, his brother Gene, Brian

Gottfried, his brother Larry, the Austins, Buster and Linda Mottram, Jimmy Connors, to name just a few.

Or there is the case of the Australians. Tennis is such a common sport that *not* to play is unusual.

In the United States it has become common for children to be playing tennis seriously from a very early age, and to receive almost daily coaching. Inevitably this produces a flood of excellent but unimaginative rote players, assembly-line products, lacking the individuality of a hand-made item.

England cannot hope to produce such a volume of high-class players, but must rely on the occasional emergence of a player who coincidentally has a proclivity for the game.

I don't think it is particularly the weather in England that is to blame as much as the poor facilities. Tennis here is still an outdoor sport and people aren't really prepared to pay to play indoors. Coaching is almost non-existent. Ex-English players would be happy to stay and coach if they were given a reasonable salary, but most go abroad because they can't make a living in England.

In America, parents raise their children from an age as early as six to play tennis. They do this even as an investment and are prepared to spend large amounts of money on lessons, etc.

There are basically two ways of getting to the top in the tennis field; one is by way of the terrific machine-like process of starting very young and the other is from a pure and natural ability.

In England, unfortunately, if a player does decide to make a career out of tennis and does have ability, there is a dearth of facilities and encouragement to-wards competitiveness. When you are selected, for say, the winter training programme, the group is pathetically small. When I was selected at the age of sixteen, I thought this was an automatic process and that *everyone* was chosen but in fact there were only about twelve of us.

In World Team Tennis* we spent many an idle moment discussing our respective backgrounds. Australian Fred Stolle first played with his parents, then in junior events. He says he wasn't particularly good or crazed about it, but everyone else was doing it, and just before he started a job as a bank clerk, he was selected for a team going abroad. With Ray Ruffels, the greatest incentive to play was getting on a team for a trip overseas. Anything to travel.

For me, my absorption in tennis was spontaneous and total. In my heart I believed I could and should be better than everyone else.

We went to Europe for about six months when I was twelve. Daddy was on an exchange visit with the Dean of Edinburgh. I immediately sneaked out to the nearest club to play. In Edinburgh there was only one

*See page 176.

other child who could give me a game, a boy younger than I. Eight years later he reminded me of our early days. He was John Clifton, one of the best Scottish players.

We also visited Rome, Geneva and Amsterdam, but returning to South Africa after the trip, for the first time I began to feel frustrations as a tennis player.

I would too often lose to the typical junior player who looped slow balls up and down the middle of the court. That type of game certainly reaches its peak at an early age. You can always learn to correct errors, but you can never acquire basic ability.

Although you might instinctively understand that in the long term, it is impossible to find any immediate consolation from it.

We played mostly on slowish courts, usually made from crushed anthills, those gigantic heaps that the ants leave behind. Also on slow cement. I didn't know the difference between slow and fast courts then, but it's obvious to me now why the slow-ballers were so successful. There I was, longing to serve and volley and hit powerfully only to be thwarted by the morphetic loops up and down the centre of the court. No wonder I started to get mad with myself when I'd miss the bloopers.

I've never been temperamental, moody or bad-tempered off the court, but when I felt I was failing on the court I couldn't tolerate it.

No one seemed to offer any constructive advice.

After a match where I'd missed a shot, then thrashed a ball as hard as I could, my teacher at school said, "Virginia, come and see me!" Obviously, I was immediately on the defensive. "Why did you slam that ball?" Well, it was pretty obvious that I did it in anger! It might have been a good question if she'd analysed the reason for the frustration and tried to give me a good enough idea for an alternate reaction.

The chain reaction started. "Virginia is erratic so we can't select her for the team." (The only team which was quite prestigious to play for.)

It was an unfortunate signature to be stuck with. You tend to give what's expected of you. Has the word ever got back to you that so and so thinks you're intelligent? The next time you're around whoever said it, you certainly don't want to do anything to dispel the myth. Or perhaps it's the opposite. People think you have a bad temper. You're not going to go out of your way to hide your feelings if you're angry because "they think I'm bad-tempered anyway, so what's the difference?" It's merely habitual reaction; there's always a choice of reaction, but who knows that at thirteen or fourteen?

My mother, whom I felt had all the answers to any of my questions and although strict was pretty sympathetic, didn't seem to take my behaviour on the court too seriously. For a start, Judy and I had done everything possible to avoid having a "tennis mother". There were plenty of those around fussing over their progeny, and we were determined to escape that embarrassment. Anyway, Mother was far too busy attending to our dietary well-being to spare the time to watch our sport (I was not weaned on porridge, but brought up on blackcurrants and cream!). She confined her interests to ferrying us to and from different courts if buses weren't available.

There was no reason anyway for her to believe I had a destructive temperament on the court. I'd never shown signs of it at home, except as she says, "Virginia had the occasional flare-up. I never knew why or how they started, but they blew over as quickly as they began!"

She had a little whip which she used as a threat against bad behaviour. I remember the impact of it only three times. Vividly!

As a child I can recall showing my temper only when I'd been punished for some misdemeanour. I'd be confined to a room, then I'd spend the next few hours trying to kick the door down.

I, personally, didn't think there was anything wrong or destructive about getting mad on the court. After all, I was angry with myself at my mistakes. I worked harder and harder, my rationale being that if I wasn't winning as much as I should I needed to spend more time on court.

Ice-skating, which for two years had been my great passion, was abandoned for tennis. Even my favourite extra gymnastics classes on Saturday afternoons gave way to a new senior membership of the tennis club.

Conveniently, the large public park adjacent to the vicarage contained a tennis club within view of the house. The quickest access was through a gap in the hedge, a method frowned on by my father, not only because it might encourage the inevitable vagrants inhabiting the park to increase their domain, but also because it wasn't too seemly for the daughter of the Archdeacon of Durban to be seen clambering through this hole.

It was too far for me to go around. I'd listen to the sound of tennis balls being hit and that was enough to give me the nerve to whip through. If I hadn't a game of my own I'd stand watching covetously. That's how I learned to serve. There was a good international player, Robin Sanders, who would spend hours practising his serve. I'd watch. Sometimes even pluck up the courage to ask if I could return it for him.

Dusk usually came too early or my practice partners ran out. Most of the other good contemporaries were less ardent than I. Their attitude was more casual, even slightly supercilious. It drove me crazy if I didn't beat them.

There was one other girl six months older than I who was good and dedicated too. It didn't exactly put my nose out of joint, but it made me doubt my unquestioned potential superiority. Till then I'd believed I could be better than any of the others, but Sally Fiore was fast and clever on the court. She thought about placing the ball. She was careful. I just wanted to bash. I was wild.

We fought for the number-one spot. Here was somebody else who really cared about the game. It was intimidating. She wasn't just good by accident; she was as devoted as I was. First it frightened, then frustrated me. Of course, my anger didn't come out directly against her, but I didn't know why it was there or how to cope with it. All I knew was that I was getting furious on the court, but I wasn't sure why. This is where more of a tennis understanding from the family could have ensured that the necessary levels of tennis were at least reached even if my emotions couldn't be entirely disciplined.

Naturally, this fracture of my self-belief led to more frustration. My panacea for any tennis problem had always been to work harder, but now I wasn't sure what to do to improve.

To add insult to injury, I was not selected for a team I'd easily made the previous year. That "rejection" really lowered my tolerance on the court. My mother even suggested that if it made me so miserable perhaps I shouldn't play!

Luckily it never quite got to that stage. Not only would I not quit that easily, but a place on the team became vacant. Getting the spot meant a lot to me, and when I played, I made sure it was well. From then on, things looked up.

There are several sifting ages in tennis. This fourteen- to fifteen-year-old period gradually sees the effectiveness of the steady reliable junior game lose its dominance over the potentially better one. It's the stage when the game with the more advanced concept begins to mature due to increasing physical strength and experience. Also, at fourteen or fifteen one is particularly vulnerable to the obvious temptations of the age, boyfriends, parties, etc. One's future priorities generally emerge at this time.

After a while Sally Fiore was no longer so keen to play. Several years later when my professional career was just beginning, she'd given up tennis to become a nun. I saw her again a few years ago when I was playing in the South African Championships in Johannesburg. She was impressed by my success and clearly idyllically happy in her vocation.

Things were beginning to move with a much more mature rhythm for me; school went well, I managed to include my daily hour of piano practice plus all my tennis.

Socially I'd gained ground too. I'd always been totally at ease with adults, but with my own age group I felt gauche and unattractive. Judy had always been a wild success with the boys. I felt precisely the younger sister; in the way and very small fry socially. Poor Judy was probably fed up enough with all my energy and then success at tennis to gloat over her social stature. But by fifteen I was going my own way, independent of her shadow and gradually acquiring some social graces of my own.

Just when this identity of mine was beginning to emerge came the shocking news that we were going to move back to England.

Daddy was highly respected and popular in Durban. His church was enormously successful, but he felt there was no further scope for him in South Africa. When he had first gone out there, racially mixed congregations had been the norm. Now the situation was changing rapidly and he was frustrated by the limits placed on the most innocuous communication between black and white. He even feared for the well-being of Bishop Zulu if their friendship became too widely known. He'd built the church up in the nine years he'd been there, and he believed it was healthy to have a change.

We understood that for his sake. We didn't understand it for ours.

I felt robbed and powerless. Now I'd have to start all over again. The only comfort in my distress was that England was the centre of the tennis world. I had always thought Wimbledon was the name of the place where tennis was played. Apparently though, it was a large suburb of London and we were, incredibly, going to be living there in a rented house. At least I wouldn't have to wait any longer for a chance to play in the famous grounds.

I was too young to enter that next June, but eighteen months later at sixteen, I made my debut as the baby of the tournament.

This was one rough I didn't have to pull myself out of. With Betty serving at 3–2 she gave me a helping hand and four straight points. That's Betty! She won her last serve to love. This one she lost to love. Her strokes are produced with a lot of wrist; she can hold the ball back till the last minute and then change direction with her wrist. It may sound like a great idea, but there's the added element of risk in this technique. The only reason she gets away with it is because she's so strong; six feet tall and tends to play a bullying type of game.

She really is quite powerful. I remember once in Perth, Australia, when we were playing the Federation Cup there, several of us—Betty, Ann and Pip Jones and some others were relaxing by the pool of the British consul. I was casually dressed (not in a swimsuit). Betty said, "Shall I throw you in the pool?" I was twenty feet from the water. I said, "Sure, go ahead," thinking I was perfectly safe. The next thing I knew was I was dangling over the water, having been swept up like a branch in a hurricane and Betty was suggesting I remove my watch. When I came up dripping I could hardly protest, just rue my naive underestimation of Betty's brawn.

She's physically stronger than she thinks. Her forte on the court is this ability to muscle the ball. My strength is more in speed and timing.

The seventh game that was coming up is the one everybody talks about as being vital; supposedly the psychological time to break serve. In fact, every game is vital, but the outlook is a little bleak if you're down 4–3 with your opponent's serve to come. At 0–40 winning my service game didn't look too promising, but as quickly as I lost the points I won them back.

On the 30–40 point I followed a good serve in and belted a high forehand which landed right inside the line for deuce. Betty walked to the umpire's chair for no ostensible reason. My ball had been way in . . . "she couldn't possibly be querying that."

It was a one-sided controversy I stayed out of: Betty likes to keep people guessing. They all thought she was questioning the line call and it turned out she was asking about a let.

Situations like these used to make people hold their breath in case it sparked off a whole incident with me. I can see how it might have done that to them, only now I had the power to choose whether to get involved or not.

It washed over me. I scarcely blinked an eye. The next two points I won easily to give me a game that had nearly been annexed by the Dutch.

We walked to towel off.

"I've got to hustle for everything . . . I hope the ballboys don't tread on my bouquets . . . I wonder how Daddy and Christopher are doing up there . . . (I had stuck them in my members' seats where I couldn't see them gnashing their teeth. My mother, sister, brother-in-law and friends were in the competitors' box.) I can just see Daddy swearing away in his unholiest way like he does when he's lost something in the house . . . you're with the wind this end . . . it'll be easier to time the ball . . . I've probably only hit 20 balls in the whole bloody match so far . . . I've got to loosen up . . . hit freely . . ."

The two ballboys at the net were collecting the old balls and sending out new ones from the refrigerator at the side of the court. That big, dark green chest doesn't look like a normal fridge, but it keeps all the balls at about 50 degrees Fahrenheit. On hot days they feel cool when they come out.

The boys were an efficient bunch, specially selected for finals day. Their uniforms always made me smile. Who would ever think of blending mauve and dark green together? Yet, I couldn't imagine Wimbledon without the fleet of ballboys attired in those colours. They were wearing old-fashioned canvas tennis shoes; that rare English breed you'd have to call plimsolls, more suitable for stealthy creeping than playing a vigorous sport.

The boy nearest me could only have been English, down to the last detail; his choirboy face, with cheeks coloured as though they'd been exposed to a cold wind, even his legs, pale with knobbly knees and little blond hairs, were almost a *national gene. Where else could you find this scene, so saturated in tradition and ritual? One I looked forward to from year to year.*

It was all so English.

At fifteen, England as a permanent home didn't have any such piquant charm for me. I suppose the basic fear was leaving my friends and the security I had so painstakingly carved out for myself.

My sadness at bidding everyone adieu was somewhat diverted by the sea voyage. I played deck sports instead of tennis, swam and ate endlessly. The one real comfort, though, was the prospect of living in Wimbledon. That alone was almost enough to subdue the misgivings I had about moving to England.

We arrived at Southampton on a cold February day in 1961. The formalities were dreary. The wait for the train to London was in a gloomy room reeking of gas from the miserable heater. Winter was hideous. My clothes were not remotely thick enough. The dream was over. This was the end of my carefree existence. Still, it would be good to see Anthony, who was at Oxford, again; Christopher, at twenty-three, had just obtained an engineering degree at the University of

Natal. And I knew that Daddy was looking forward to taking up his post as General Secretary for the United Society for Christian Literature, the Lutterworth Press.

Durban might not have been the epitome of rural life; it was, after all, a large city. But no one in a hot climate moves too fast. From the atmosphere of languorous heat it was an abrupt change to the winter of England.

The crowds all hurried in the London chill. They didn't have time to smile at strangers. For the first time in my life I felt isolated.

Even the house we were staying in was the dullest on the street. Somehow all the others were nice except for this one which was probably rented because nobody wanted to live in it permanently.

I escaped the next morning to look for the tennis courts. At the top of the hill, I passed a church with a tall slim spire looking as though it came straight off an English post card. No wonder the street was called Church Road.

I couldn't quite see the courts, only an enormous triangular area surrounded by a concrete wall, hedges and trees. At the end was the main building of the stadium. As I got lower my vantage point wasn't so good and besides I couldn't wait any longer so I ran the last hundred yards.

When I got there the wrought-iron gates were open, but there was a sign saying "Private". I didn't know what to do. I was dying to go in. I stood and stared for a while then edged my way up a few yards but I was just too timid to go far enough to see it all. How I wished I could see what grass courts looked like and the electric scoreboard where the players had their scores flashed up in lights. I wished someone friendly would come along and ask me if I'd like to be shown around.

Finally I got cold and left. I walked up the hill with a sinking feeling in the pit of my stomach. Now I'd seen Wimbledon I didn't have anything to look forward to. The one thing that had kept me going for weeks was over in fifteen minutes.

The next and only thing to do was to look for courts where I could play, winter or not.

There were public courts near our house and eventually Judy and I joined the club opposite the All England Club. In junior tournaments I started off with success, walking through my age group and nearly winning the under-eighteens.

In between tennis I had to go to Wimbledon Grammar School. For the first time the term "depression" took on a particular meaning for me. I don't believe I learned a thing that summer. There was no reason to try. I was too homesick to find any motivation to do schoolwork.

I guess when people are unhappy they look for a life raft. For some it's religion. For others, hobbies. For Judy it was probably a boyfriend. She was actually in a worse position than I. She'd already matriculated in South Africa but had to go back for another year to get the A-levels necessary for a teacher training course.

My salvation was tennis.

I played all the available tournaments, the public parks and the schoolgirls and won them all. The summer wasn't too bad as long as it wasn't raining.

When the time for Wimbledon arrived I was too young to enter, but watching daily was a high point for me. When I couldn't acquire tickets, I'd wait till after school and five o'clock when the cheap tickets went on sale. If I couldn't persuade anyone to go with me I'd go alone. Now when I wonder how all those people stand to watch I tend to forget I did exactly the same thing. The length of the line waiting for standing room on the Centre Court was little discouragement. I wanted to get in and I stayed until the last match was over or called off on account of darkness.

Naturally enough, my favourites were South Africans. Sandra Reynolds and Renée Schuurman did well in the doubles that year. I was their biggest fan. After all, I'd ball-girled for them lots of times in Durban and had managed to acquire their autographs more than once. There was also Cliff Drysdale, the nineteen-year-old wonder boy.

There was no television in South Africa. I'd never seen international tennis stars play, but their names

With Sally Holdsworth at the 1962 Junior Covered Court Championships

An early indoor match at Queen's Club, one of the first photographs to appear in print

Maureen Connolly, after winning
her last Wimbledon Ladies' Final,
1954

With Teddy Tinling, who had
designed her dresses throughout
her career, and Frances MacLennan
(now Taylor)

were familiar through newspapers and magazines. Wimbledon was my first contact with them. Instead of wondering what they were doing at the other end of the world, I was actually in the same place at the same time. I knew when they were on court. I could see them walking up to the competitors' buffet or climbing into the limousines at the club entrance, and if I spoke to them they would have to know I existed, if only for a split second.

In the final that year 1961, Christine Truman lost to Angela Mortimer in a very controversial match. Christine was a set up (there had been a forty-minute delay due to rain) and within a point of leading 5–3 in the second when she slipped and fell. There was a lot of hypothesising about what would have happened if she hadn't. Would Christine have sustained her lead or would Angela have been able, as she had on other occasions, to come steadily from behind to beat Christine? Angela won, but she never got full credit for that match. She retired shortly after that, but did go on to captain the Wightman Cup team.

I wasn't sure how I felt about it. It was all a little muddled. Poor Christine falling over just when things were looking brightest for her and yet, fancy Angela winning Wimbledon and having her greatest moment flawed by an uncertainty.

Anyway, the moment the presentation was over I rushed through the debating crowd on their way to the tea lawns. My destination, powered by my first real savour of Wimbledon's magic, was the courts over the road to get ready for next year's final!

We moved to Tunbridge Wells that same summer. I had two more years left at school before university.

In the winter on Saturdays and Sundays with books in tow, I'd drag up to London by train to practise at Queen's Club. There was organised winter training for the best juniors with George Worthington, the popular Australian coach.

I didn't have very much in common with the others. They were all slightly older and had abandoned school to concentrate solely on tennis. I felt rather lumpish; the pig-tailed schoolgirl still in uniform, naive, un-conversant with big city life. Still, being the butt of their good-natured jokes didn't dampen my eagerness to get on the indoor courts to play those precious couple of hours.

If there was a tournament anywhere within reach by train, I'd beg time off from school to play. Any qualms Miss Hazell, my headmistress, might have had about allowing me were dispelled when I qualified for Wimbledon and when we won the Abedare Cup in 1962, an inter-school competition. This was a great win, the first ever by a grammar school.

By this time I was supposed to be the most promising junior in England. The press were beginning to take notice of me. The "tempestuous" trend they were never to let up on, started in England that year when I played a girl a couple of years my senior at Hurlingham.

Carole Rosser was very attractive; tall and thin with raven black hair. She not only had a quick temper, but used words which had never found a place in my cloistered background.

Someone once told me a story about two very *very* elderly English ladies watching a match of Carole's. Evidently she flew off the handle over something, and out came a torrent of, shall we say, indecorous language. The ladies stared . . . it was difficult to know just what they thought. One old woman looked at the other and behaving every inch the unimpeachable source, said, "See, I told you she was foreign." Such was the esoteric potential of Carole's language.

We were close in standard, and our match was quite a tussle. As I recall, she lost her calm first, then I began to take more liberties. Between the two of us it was a spectacle of foot stamping, racquet throwing and screaming. It's a wonder we didn't blacken each other's eyes.

We did behave badly then, and that's the way it should have been called, but from that day on, no matter how well I behaved, all that came up was my reputation for a temper. You can't just chastise someone for getting angry. It only makes it worse. There were plenty of boring stuffed-shirts who reprimanded me without any intelligent understanding.

On one occasion during a school match without any umpire or overseer, Judy and I were cheated outrageously on several calls by the opposition. There happened to be a member of the Kent Lawn Tennis Association watching from a distance who didn't see the cheating but saw my reaction to it. Afterwards in front of a whole group, he told me in his officious way that my behaviour was disgraceful. His humiliating me so indiscreetly only added to my frustration. I have never forgotten the incident nor forgiven his sententious moralising, especially as nowadays he is the most anxious to kiss me when I do well.

Once my "temperament" was latched onto, I became so conscious of my behaviour I'd be unable to think properly during a match. If I missed an easy shot I'd get furious, then waste time trying to control my anger and miss another easy shot. Getting mad made me feel guilty, and suppressing myself scuttled my involvement in the match.

While I wouldn't exactly have called myself stubborn, I was a strong-willed young lady. If I respected or liked someone their criticism was accepted, but if not I went my own way. It was Billie Jean King who, a year or so later, gave me the best advice. "You never have time on the court to waste getting mad." Coming from an outsider it probably would have landed on stony ground, but from a good player it meant something.

As I was finishing my A-levels in pure and applied

maths and physics, knowing the answer would be "No", I suggested to my parents having a year off to play tennis full-time. Eighteen was the age to concentrate on getting the experience of international competition. Champions started blooming soon after, and that's what I had in mind.

The English educational system may have some brilliant aspects, but asking mere children to choose between arts and science is absurd in its prematurity. At fifteen, maths satisfied me totally. It was a few years later as my relationship with the outside world began developing that I doubted its suitability to my personality. By then it was too late to change.

My interests were increasingly in the cultural sphere. It was more interesting for me to converse about music, art, sports, people, human relationships, etc. than about maths. They offered more opportunity for imagination and creativity.

Besides, university maths is so advanced that it reaches a rarefied stratum; so abstract that it no longer bears any direct connection to human behaviour.

Several times I was seriously tempted to quit studying. There was no one to practise with in Brighton. The compromise was an arduous train ride to London.

There was no real interest in tennis at the university either. Sport was rather out of fashion. Sussex was the first of the red-brick universities with a reputation for being avant-garde. Old establishment principles were replaced by liberal attitudes. Tennis fell into the former classification. Having endured years of compulsory sport at school no one wanted anything to do with it now.

I was even embarrassed to be seen with racquets. In the summer time an undergraduate carrying one grungy old racquet, symbolising tennis of a social nature, would have been just about permissible. To have several, and in mid-winter, bore the stigma of unacceptable seriousness.

But my racquets could no longer be concealed. I had been a promising top-ranked junior long enough. My potential had to be borne out.

George Worthington, the coach in my first days of Lawn Tennis Association training, was one of my supporters.

At the British Junior Championships at Wimbledon in 1962 the year before, I was seeded No 1 but lost dismally to a girl called Wendy Hall. She was a limited player who only pushed the ball back, but she was intelligent. The conditions were rainy and heavy. Instead of adapting to them, I took more and more chances, vainly trying to hit my way through the match. It ended quicker than I thought possible. It hadn't entered my mind that unless I changed my game I'd lose.

The conservative talent scouts put it this way: "It's no good having the biggest and best-looking shots if you can't place them accurately." George couldn't really argue, but no one could stop him from thinking, "Wait and see."

A few months later we were on fast courts for the final of the Junior Indoor Championships with Mary McAnally as my opponent. There was no reason to lose, but I did. I never divulged why. To my shame, it was simply overconfidence that lost me that match.

This time the tennis cognoscenti judged, "It's no use! She's got no control of the ball." George's answer: "They give me a belly-ache. There's a girl who would be a world beater and because she can't win junior tournaments they lose faith in her. One day she'll prove I'm right."

George had been a great player himself; he had an eye for spotting talent. The others were the ones who couldn't make it on the court so they became "critical experts" off the field.

My results did begin to consolidate somewhat in those university years. In the spring I would trundle off to play on the French Riviera circuit, always carrying my books which were beginning to feel grafted to me. After the monotony of long winter training, I was gushing over with pent-up energy and impatient for my deliverance to the outdoors.

The Riviera was beautiful. The competition on the slow European clay was about the right standard. There was a chance to win tournaments, but one had good players like Gail Sheriff and Helga Niessen to overcome.

Although accompanied by other young British players such as Robin Blakelock, Stanley Matthews, Graham Stillwell and Frances MacLennan, socially it was a little lonely. It's such a handicap not speaking the language. Unfortunately, my French never improved, but I did learn to conjugate thirty-six verbs in charades.

Everything seemed so expensive. The Riviera isn't exactly made for penniless students; all that glorious French food, but only enough money to eat the simplest. We were on a minimal grant from the LTA to help us out. Mind you, it was better for me not to be able to eat too much. All winter at university, with mealtimes as the highlights of the day, did nothing for my shape. Till then I'd always eaten as much as I could and been skinny. At Sussex my figure expanded with each mouthful of cafeteria food I ate. I was never fat, but solid, so to speak. It's such a relief when one's body finally stabilises in the mid-twenties.

Just as I was beginning to feel the wings of freedom I'd have to return to university bondage. We'd set off in all directions; the full-timers for the likes of Rome and Paris, the students back to the secret lore of physics lectures and blackboard scrawl.

It was my second Wightman Cup in 1966 but my first on home ground. I was proud of my ascent to the

No 2 ranking in Great Britain. Although the event coincided exactly with my finals, there was no question in my mind that I would still represent my country in the match. Although there were enough students on the verge of nervous breakdowns from the strain of exams alone, that did not put me off.

Against the recommendation of school advisers, a room was set up for me right in Wimbledon so I could walk straight from exams to the tennis.

Half my mind was on the court. The other half struggling through questions about nuclear physics and abstract mathematics. Doubtless, the answers were even more abstract as my concentration fluctuated between tennis and maths theories; usually the latter on court and the former at the desk.

Our team was faring extraordinarily well. We were 3–1 up against the Americans and needed only one more match to win the Cup. I was next to play Nancy Richey. The odds were heavily in favour of Nancy, hot from reaching the final of Paris, to beat me.

As I got to 5–3 in the third set and within 3 points of the title I didn't want to look anywhere near the cup shining at the side of the court.

My legs turned to jelly. All the aces I'd been serving started missing by inches, and Nancy tenaciously hung on to win 7–5.

3–2. We had yet another chance. Ann was to play Billie Jean and looked headed for victory when Billie Jean developed cramp in her leg. The interruption in momentum was enough to distract Ann into losing.

The doubles was next to go down the tube, and we lost the match.

I was exhausted. The following day as I sat staring at exam questions which I couldn't even understand, let alone answer, my mind kept harking back to 5–3 and 15–0. I must have replayed that game a hundred times.

Each time the summer semester was over it felt as though I'd been unlaced from a whalebone corset. Unfortunately Wimbledon usually started the next day. There wasn't even twenty-four hours to prepare.

I was the most widely publicised British player. Christine Truman had held the hopes of the home public high for so long but was past her peak. Though Ann reached the semifinals of Wimbledon each year, her game was like a cake without the final layer of icing.

Mine had too much icing and not enough cake. The press and public pinned their hopes on me all the same and built up my chances of doing well. They weren't seriously thinking of me as a Wimbledon champ, but knew I could hit a streak on a day and beat anyone. Conjuring up the possibility tickled them.

From my own point of view, I too was hoping I'd be lucky. My appearances there as a schoolgirl had been more than encouraging. The first year, having survived the qualifying event, I'd won a round and lost only in three hard sets to Judy Tegart, a good

Australian. The following year, on my Centre Court debut, I played above myself, pushing Ann Haydon.

Those two years I played on complete inspiration for the occasion. Foolishly, I thought Wimbledon's galvanising effect would be all I'd ever need to win.

I fancied the magnified expectation of me. It supported my own personal crusade to prove that combining university and tennis was not an outré idea. Teachers in school and then professors insisted it was impossible for me to do both. Their arbitrary presumption to decide my future and the belittlement of tennis made me unable to resist trying to show they were wrong.

They had one valid point though, which was obscured to me by my prejudice. If I was at university there just wasn't adequate time to prepare for good results at Wimbledon.

Accordingly, the three Wimbledons I played during my university years of 1964, 1965 and 1966, didn't meet the general reckoning. The evaluation of the press was that I had Wimbledon jitters and didn't have a big match temperament.

It was a tailor-made excuse; my nerves were to blame. The last thing I wanted to do was admit that the academics might have been close to the truth. It was easier to go along with the "conventional wisdom".

It became a fait-accompli.

Instead of accepting that my negligible results were

due to lack of preparation and fallible technique, so I could start again from first principles, I began to conform to the role that had been written for me.

This way, it took me years to unravel the tangled skein of this complexity. Success at Wimbledon requires virtually a twelve-month preparation. You need to harness your energies in order to convert them into an asset. Somehow I thought providence would see that it all just happened.

Suffice it to say I lost the next two games.

I felt the weight of the Royal glare on my shoulders. "Poor Queen . . . she makes this big effort to come to a tennis match which she can't stand and she has to sit through this . . . they'll all throw that quote back at me . . ." (After I'd beaten Chris and every second question was, "How will you feel playing in front of the Queen?" I'd said that I'd hoped to convert her to tennis.) "This will convert her all right . . . she won't come back till the next Jubilee . . ."

I could just hear some dippy reporter from an obscure tennis biannual calling me a wounded lioness while the others sat in conclave over the riddle of my atavism.

I mean, for heaven's sake, this match hadn't even started

for me yet. I just wasn't worried at all. I had the feeling that I'd like to hold up a sign saying, "Listen everybody, don't panic. Everything will be all right."

At 4–5 down it didn't seem I was going about it in a very direct manner; still, I was so sure I would win. I felt the crowd's faith in me, but knew their hopes had been dashed so many times they must be feeling twinges of uncertainty.

As for all the people in front of their televisions at home, I had visions of them escaping into the kitchen to make a cup of tea. Or perhaps they preferred the therapeutic exercise of gardening to the emotional callisthenics of watching a Ginny Wade match.

How well I know that feeling when you desperately want someone to win. I used to feel so physically ill when Anthony, my elder brother, was playing squash, or Christopher running a race, that I almost couldn't watch. Or with friends in tennis if you come along when they're winning and suddenly they start losing, you feel solely responsible.

I could almost see the TV sets fading and dying, switched off by tremulous hands as that smash Betty hit broke my serve to give her 5–4.

Most of my family were there watching in person. They'd been toughened by years of experience and could endure a few setbacks.

But what about those devoted fans? How were they bearing up?

Mr Andrea, my favourite restaurateur in London, nearly wept when I reached the final. In his emotional

77

Greek way he promised me a feast prepared by his own hands when I won. I could imagine him sitting there in Charlotte Street paying less attention to his patrons than to my fortunes on the television.

Down in Faversham the village had probably ground to a complete standstill. Mr Jackson, the fishmonger, promised to give me an entire salmon. And Mr Neaves, the neighbouring farmer, had offered a gift of what are unquestionably the most luscious strawberries in the country.

One person who would be positive through thick and thin was Fred, the gardener. I could hear him saying, "Come on, Ginny . . . that's the way . . . she can't win too quickly . . . we want a little entertainment." Fred Ward is the one man my parents couldn't do without at Sharsted, their house.

About ten years ago when the family was splitting up through marriages and careers, my parents were left rattling around in their home in Tunbridge Wells. At first it seemed contradictory to move to Sharsted, an edifice more like a village with its seventy odd rooms, but it was on sale for a song. While Anthony was designing the University of Kent down in Canterbury, he came across it and it seemed perfect for him and his family to have one section and my parents another.

There is so much space, equivalent to about four very large houses, that you might never see another person for days. It is really quite magnificent with sections dating back to medieval times and the rest seventeenth-century Jacobean. It's versatile in its range for whatever taste one has. The formality is there if you choose it, yet there is available informality. When any of my friends come down, I have to prepare them not to be unstrung by the grand appearance of the outside. Our basis for living is really a simple country existence.

There is always an exploratory jaunt to go on. My nieces and nephews are eternally amused by expeditions up and down unused staircases, in and out of hidden rooms, into the attics or cellar or racing round some of the enormous rooms in toy cars. There's always a willing guide too. No one, least of all my father, ever tires of chaperoning a tour.

Personally, I like the stables most of all. Downstairs are the relics of a coach-and-four era, with enough stalls to accommodate a score of horses and milk a herd of cows. Above, the rooms that slept stable boys and servants are the sunniest and best proportioned of the entire house. They're neglected now but ready to come to life at anyone's behest, as is the barn, where there hasn't been hay for much too long. We may not be living in grand style but we thrive in its peaceful nonconformity, and preserve it from land developers or dilapidation.

The ballroom was built for someone's 21st birthday in about 1900. The last time we had a gathering fit for a room of such proportions was my 21st.

My mother spent days creating an exotic spread of food. She's always good with large numbers of people to feed. This time she had one hundred plus. John Macdonald, a

New Zealand ex-tennis player came down with his band. It didn't rain and there was a beautiful sunset to make everyone forget it was chilly. Anthony made a speech about me. We drank plenty of champagne, a few bottles of which still remain nostalgically in the cellar. It was quite an occasion.

While Anthony was speaking about me, I thought, "Now if I had just won Wimbledon I would really be able to justify everyone's attention on me and enjoy myself. When I win Wimbledon I must have another celebration!"

I was a break down at 4–5 with Betty serving for the first set. The previous time I'd lost my serve at 2–2 I immediately won hers back, but on grass against a player with a big serve, you cannot reasonably expect to break too often. It's not like slower courts, clay or some indoor synthetic surfaces, where the advantage of the server is neutralised and breaks happen as often as not.

There was a possibility Betty might be a trifle edgy serving for the set. Also, I felt looser, on the verge of hitting my stride. I was finally beginning to perspire which meant the adrenalin was at last starting to flow.

As I faced the onslaught I gave myself two clear plans of attack. If I could, I would break and endeavour to push home the advantage. If she came up with too many good shots and I lost the game, I would simultaneously be preparing for the opening game of the second set, then be ready to forge ahead, while she might temporarily be experiencing a lapse, having just won the set.

Virginia and Billie Jean King after Virginia's famous win at the Forest Hills final in 1968

With Ann Jones during a Dewar Cup tournament in 1970

With actress Nyree Dawn Porter and singer Lulu before attending a Women of the Year Luncheon at the Savoy

Lesley Hunt, Virginia, Patti Hogan and Caroline Battrick pictured at the 1971 Monte Carlo Show

The first serve was a let. I made the shot anyway. She served again, right down the centre-line. I could hardly get my racquet on it. My only antidote to this type of serving was inspiration and instinct but that didn't start working till later on.

The next serve I returned invitingly high, but it produced an error from Betty. 15–15.

My following return was better, but nonetheless treated disdainfully with a winning backhand volley from Betty. 30–15.

Now she was being very deliberate with her preparation to serve; bouncing the ball several times, sort of cocking and aiming the racquet, loosening her shoulders.

There are idiosyncratic mannerisms that each player has. The general effect of any of them is to get you balanced with a clear picture in your mind where you're serving and with whichever selected spin. Then you can swing freely. Mostly everyone bounces the ball several times, mainly to collect oneself or sometimes to catch one's breath. Some players always bounce it the same number of times, like Sue Barker or Raul Ramirez; others almost in direct proportion to the importance of the point, like Jimmy Connors.

Betty doesn't look where she's going to serve. She seems to keep her eyes glued on the ground by the baseline. I don't look at the exact spot but into the entire service box.

She took her time. The serve came to my forehand. We had a long rally, about the first one since the opening game. I kept the ball deep and managed to get in to the net to hit a winning backhand volley.

That was more my style. That point perked me up no end. The crowd sensed it too, and clapped happily.

Even more deliberate over the next important point at 30 all, she went for her favourite serve down the middle. It was a few inches long. While she walked slowly back for her second serve I kept moving; little dance steps up and down on my toes.

Sometimes I want to keep mobile; in this match I still needed more exertion. Other times I'm calmer and more composed. Some days you have to keep bolstering yourself up and others just the reverse, making yourself relax. I never feel the same two days in a row. It's one of the reasons tennis is so creative. You have to be alert each moment; recognising nuances of moods, physical or mental, and be ready to adapt for the appropriate play or reaction.

The second serve was edgy enough for a double fault and break-point for me. Betty mopped her brow with her forearm and wiped her hand on her dress. Hands are inclined to get a little damper at 30–40.

I was ready for the next point. It was a chance for me to even it up at 5–5. I slapped my thigh and muttered to myself to watch the ball, be ready. I was on my toes.

Fault. I stood aggressively inside the baseline. But here was the irony of Betty's serve again. Having dished up a double to be 30–40 and with a fault first serve you'd have to expect a more cautious approach, but she just whacked it and it went in for a good serve. I just missed the backhand down the line. It wasn't the most sensible shot to try. I'd blown a model set-up for a break; I'd failed to return a

82

second serve in court at 30–40. *That sort of thing infuriates my sense of perfection about this game. Even if you aren't playing in top form there are certain cardinal rules you must comply with, and one is to return a second serve in court.*

I walked to the right court, disgusted with that shot. I couldn't stand making elementary errors. That strong feeling of displeasure was enough to obliterate any remaining inhibitions caused by nerves.

At deuce I did my best but was beaten by a better shot. With Betty on the verge of winning the set there was grudging applause.

The next point I scrambled back three or four balls and had an opening for a winning backhand volley to save set point, but I put it straight onto her racquet and lost the point.

The scoreboard flickered like a pinball machine. With a flurry of lights, the little silver ball had escaped through the gap. The arrangement of lights came to rest showing a 4 by Wade and a 6 by the name Stove with an extra bonus of 1 under sets.

I felt no qualms. I had tried to get the first set over with too quickly and had rushed it. Now, after forty minutes, I knew I'd have to stay out there a lot longer; all afternoon if necessary. With all respect for Betty there was no way I was leaving that court the loser. I was going to get to use the Royal etiquette we'd been briefed on just before the match.

Earlier, at precisely 1.45, the phone in the dressing room had rung. Mrs Fraser, the lady who looks after the players, relayed the message that Betty and I were to go downstairs to the Centre Court waiting room. There were about six other people in the dressing room at the time, all bustling with excitement, making an occasion of the day, almost to the point where Betty and I had become accessories.

We collected our racquets and towels. I took an orange because I always get hungry on the court. We had two bouquets each; one from Fred Hoyles, the referee, and one in the club colours of mauve and green from the secretary and committee of the All England Club. The tags were the same for both of us. "Betty, Good Luck." "Virginia, Good Luck."

We were so laden down that Mrs Fraser and her pre-decessor Mrs Twynham helped carry our flowers. Mrs Twynham had retired only two years before, after attending to our every need ever since I'd been an honoured member of that dressing room. She came back once or twice during the championships. I was pleased to see her. She was emotional as we left the dressing room and walked along the short corridor which leads into the main club reception rooms. "I wish I was still here," she said. "This is what I wanted." In 1974 when I'd lost in the semifinal to Olga Morozova, she'd whispered to me in commiseration that she couldn't retire until I won the tournament.

As one enters the landing there is a photograph on the opposite wall of the Queen presenting the trophy to the men's doubles winners one of the previous times she'd been there, and there is an oil portrait of Princess Marina. It is always quiet in this foyer except when tea is being served to

84

the occupants of the Royal Box. I usually keep my eyes down in case I should meet some VIP and have to make an embarrassed greeting. There were scores there on finals day, although I knew they would not be floating about, as the Royal group was still in the members' enclosure having luncheon.

The staircase is elegantly carpeted in pale green. The banister leading into the main room of the club always glistens with polish. Each day as I'd walked down I'd noticed the spectacular flower display. This time it was an array of redolent white lilies and sprays. On the wall above the flowers hang the rolls of honour with the names of all the previous champions. Flanking the other side is the glass display cabinet where all the trophies are exhibited. Now the centrepiece, the ladies singles' salver, was missing, probably having a last-minute buff for its annual outing. Above the door is the wooden plaque inscribed in gold letters with Kipling's quotation, "If you can meet with triumph and disaster and treat those two impostors just the same."

I didn't feel particularly different on my way to play the final of Wimbledon. Somehow all those years I'd dreamed about it, I'd expected to walk down those stairs feeling a rush through my veins. But here I was, just the usual me thinking the usual thoughts before a match. If anything was different, there was mild numbness of my senses. I had been more excited about flying in Concorde the first time!

Sitting alone with your opponent in the little room behind the Centre Court is one of the most awkward preliminaries to playing a Centre Court match. If possible I wait until the last minute to go there. This time I knew there would be ten minutes to endure as we waited for the Queen, without even a chance to sneak back to the dressing room to pay a last call to the loo.

This waiting room is indelibly etched in my mind. Each time I'm there I notice a sort of ritual that both players act out. Someone will head for a deceptively comfortable looking divan next to the wall. Without fail there are a few expletives on impact. It's not soft at all, but the choice is either that or an equally inhospitable wicker chair.

Conversation gets somewhat desultory so the next move is for someone to examine the cartoon dated 1925 on the wall. On it there is caricatured a group of people in varying degrees of prostration at the discovery of a dandelion on the Centre Court. It was amusing ·at first, but when you've scrutinised every grain of it dozens of times the entertainment value wears thin.

That's when you flick through the two or three magazines lying on the small glass-topped table. The words mean nothing. Who cares about the fashions in Vogue *or which president is being bear-hugged by Brezhnev? But over the course of the tournament the pages still become bent and smudged by twitchy hands.*

It seemed forever, waiting with Betty and Peter Morgan, the man who makes sure we're there and sends us out on the court. To the strains of "Land of Hope and Glory" we were instructed on proper conduct for the Queen.

It was such a long time that I resigned myself to talking rather than sitting silently. "So you don't speak until you're spoken to, and the first time you say 'Your Majesty' and the second time 'Ma'am', right?" Betty said, "In Holland, we say 'Madam' the second time." We repeated it back and forth so many times that in the end I didn't know if you were allowed to talk at all. My mind was miles away. There were enough extraneous thoughts tugging at my concentration without worrying whether I'd trip over my shoelaces when I curtsied.

I'd never been introduced to the Queen. The nearest I'd been was at Sussex when she paid the university a visit one Friday. We spent days speculating whether she'd remove the fish bones from her mouth with her fork or her fingers. I won't say what she did.

Most of the other members of the Royal Family I'd met briefly at one time or another and had been charmed.

One finals day during a luncheon at the All England Club I had the honour of meeting Princess Margaret, who is a keen tennis spectator. "Virginia," she said, "I just love the way you throw the ball up to serve and it hangs suspended in the air until you choose to hit it." I liked her. She is full of personality and verve.

The Duke and Duchess of Kent and Prince Michael are all delightful. One winter when I was the guest of my godmother in Switzerland, I skied with the Duke. With those long legs he went at such a lick I had to use every ounce of my tennis muscles to keep up.

When I first tried I was crazy about skiing. Then as I became more conscious of the repercussions if I injured myself, I skied with less speed and more caution. It gave me reason to forego my competitiveness and indulge in a sport purely for pleasure. Skiing with the Duke left me a little breathless. I was quite happy to arrive at the bottom of the mountain behind him and, more importantly, whole.

When I was invested with my MBE at Buckingham Palace in 1973 the Queen was in Australia so the Queen Mother presided.

There was so much instruction on etiquette before the affair that I feared a stultifying formality in the hush of the Royal Gallery. Once I'd curtsied, though, the rest had an aura of intimacy. She stood benignly on a dais making her the same height as I was on the ground, and conversed seeming to know all about me.

I felt sorry for the lady behind me, next in line for her moment of recognition. A curtsy·can be a totally unfamiliar position for a body, especially when butterflies in the stomach have a most unbalancing effect. She performed her contortion, and with her eyes on the Queen Mother, walked forward to be greeted. On her third step, she kicked the podium and lost her balance, virtually falling right into the sympathetic arms of Her Majesty. I'm sure it created, in the heads of all who had seen it, monstrous images of themselves slipping and skating across the floor.

As for the Queen, I knew nothing more about her than most other people did; only what could be read; she's a family-orientated person, loves horses, isn't interested in tennis and has a great sense of humour. Apparently, once when she was visiting in the Bahamas, her host took a silver pencil out of his pocket and proceeded to swizzle the bubbles *out of a drink. The Queen remarked, "Well, that's all right in our company, but what happens when you're in High Society?"*

Peter Morgan was in quite a state over the whole affair. He kept peering outside the door to see whether the blue light was on signifying royalty in the stands directly above us.

He didn't need to look. At exactly 1.57, two minutes ahead of schedule, the crowd let out a thunderous burst of applause to greet the Queen and then rose to its feet to join with the orchestra in the National Anthem.

I knew I'd have to use the etiquette lesson after the match, but I didn't want to think further than the initial curtsy on the service line as we went into battle.

A twenty-first birthday is supposed to be the theoretical milestone in one's maturity. I don't know whether celebrating mine did serve to baptise me for a loftier position in life. I do know that early the next morning after my party, I left numerous friends still sleeping in whichever of the ample rooms they'd chosen on whatever meagre form of bedding they could find, to fly to the US convinced that I was heading straight for the top of the tennis tree.

I gave myself two years to capture the tennis golden fleece. After that I'd be anxious to settle down at some steady consequential job, marry an impressive man, and be a thoroughly regular member of society.

What, in fact, ensued, was a two-year period of confusion in myself and my tennis endeavours.

Naturally there was a stage of readjustment from the previous dual existence as an undergraduate and a tennis player. During the latter part of university when I was under considerable time pressure and stress, I just kept going, clinging to the knowledge that it would soon end. There hadn't been a moment to relax and take stock of myself. I became used to just rushing from one thing to another.

When the pressure ended, I wasn't accustomed to spare time, let alone using it constructively in a self-exploratory way. Habitually I still felt the obligation to use every minute actively. When I wasn't playing matches or practising I had to be sightseeing, meeting new people or doing something new. The more I did, the more I saw, the more parties I went to, the better.

If there were let-downs, I looked for activity to distract me. Depression was almost forbidden. I believed I had so many positive things going for me that I had no right to be depressed for long.

Off the court people would see me with a self-assured deportment, but there was none of the calm that comes when one finally connects with oneself.

On the court my turmoil was impossible to conceal. How could I win consistently when my play reflected the mood of each particular day? The anticipation of being a full-time tennis player wasn't matched by the real thing. I had a surge of better results but then the newness paled and the old problems remained.

Subtle changes had been creeping into my feelings about tennis. Looking for my *raison d'être,* where did hitting tennis balls come into it? The demands were great and the rewards elusive.

It was as if I purposely refused to analyse the question of winning. In the middle of a tough match, if I asked myself, "Do you want to win?" there was usually a blank for an answer. There were enough moments of success to allow me to bluff myself that I was making adequate progress.

My biggest mistake was not fully committing myself to a realistic challenge, never openly tackling the reason why I wasn't winning enough. Instead I began to be convinced that concentrating so solely on this one tennis goal would result in my being boring or lopsided. Physically I continued to butt my head uselessly against the wall, while mentally I stayed out of it.

Aspiration and reality should be a viable amalgamation; the initial vision fused with the day-to-day spade work. For me they spelled confusion. I had no idea how to go about directing my energies to give them more of a prismatic effect; I couldn't comprehend the unity of mental and physical efforts.

For many years I was to keep them almost mutually exclusive.

The tennis circuit was very international in those days. There was the opportunity to travel almost anywhere. My first stop was California. Previous years I had watched enviously as everybody headed West after Forest Hills. Finally I could, too. I wasn't disappointed. We spent a week on the beach in La Jolla, supposedly practising but usually too drugged by sun and swimming to make more than a token effort.

There was a fourteen-year-old girl there who was supposed to be the most talented young player around. She was skinny with a bright cheery face and always wore a straw boater with badges all over it. She was good, but she had a temper on the court that made me look sedated! This was Patti Hogan.

In LA the next week Winnie Shaw and I were beating her in doubles and were absolutely transfixed by her tears and tantrums. Watching other people go berserk on the court was a most salutary exercise for me. I could watch impartially while they illustrated quite how pointless it was. Patti was a very talented player who never learned how to restrain herself.

Initially, Los Angeles was a bewildering city of expansive proportions. How people operated without the feeling of a community nucleus I wasn't sure. It was so different from other big cities, as if a handful of pebbles had been thrown in all directions and each one had become a mini-city within the actual Los Angeles city limit. One absolutely had to have a car to traverse the distances. No one thought anything of hopping in the car and driving forty miles on the incredibly efficient freeways just to see a movie.

The air in Los Angeles was a mess. There was more smog there in 1966 than there is now. Playing tennis with streaming, smarting eyes was not easy, not that I ended up playing that much. Winnie and I did win the doubles in the Pacific Southwest, but my singles was a disaster. I was put on a remote back court without an umpire, ballboys or even an inch of space where an adventurous spectator might stand. Not only was I hating every lonesome minute of this match, searching in vain for a good reason to be there, but to add to my disgust, my opponent was cheating on calls. By habit I struggled on. I was in such a state, though, there was no way I could win.

The rest of the week I despised myself. As I hadn't acquired anything from the tennis, I endeavoured to cram in whatever else I could, from Disneyland and movie sets to crossing the Mexican border where I was tempted to stay, I was so aggravated by losing that match.

The tournament no longer exists for the women. A couple of years after my visit it was the scene of one of the events which motivated women's tennis into going its own successful way. Jack Kramer helped promote the now obsolete tournament. He was never much of an admirer of the ladies, underestimating their performances and refusing equal prize money with the men.

Billie Jean and Rosie were playing in the final. They were apparently beset by so many bad calls and weren't happy with the way the referee handled it, that they both refused to continue and walked off the court.

I didn't see the incident. I spoke to Rosie about it recently and she summarised it this way:

". . . I'm a set up and have a point for a break. There's a bad call from a lineswoman who's been making all these mistakes. The whole thing blows up. The 'Old Lady' fumes and walks off the court. I went off, too. There was no way I was going to stand out there and get the match awarded to me that way . . ."

After that, without overtly prohibiting the girls from playing the tournament, Jack Kramer certainly influenced their decision by offering them only a fraction of the prize-money the men received. Under the guidance of Gladys Heldman the girls retaliated with a sortie which was to pave the way for women's tennis of today.

Philip Morris has already had a major interest in tennis, and Virginia Slims was a recent brand of cigarettes that specialised in using Women's Lib as a basis for their advertising campaign. Gladys persuaded them to become involved as a sponsor.

They started with a group of girls who signed a contract for the grand sum of $1. For a year there was rivalry amongst the Virginia Slims contract pros and the others. Then I too joined the circuit; liked it, but wasn't prepared to be on the road for months on end. In those days, based in London, I hated being away for more than five weeks at a time.

Gladys expected me to play non-stop. A disagreement about my commitments was inevitable.

The United States Tennis Association also had a circuit which I then became part of, along with players like Chris Evert, Evonne Goolagong, and Martina Navratilova. The stars of the Virginia Slims circuit were Billie Jean King, Rosie Casals and Margaret Court. These two tours operated separately until 1974 when the opposing sides united, realising that factions were even less effective than one strong tour. Virginia Slims were the overall sponsor.

Now, nearly a decade after the original breakaway, the progress of women's tennis is obvious with the still burgeoning success of the Virginia Slims circuit and other events. It was quite a jump, but the girls landed on their feet.

From the sunshine of California I returned to the damp, cold autumn of England where there were brave efforts to start a few indoor tournaments. Playing in Stalybridge, Cheshire, where the courts were set up in a vacated cold warehouse and the rain dripped through holes in the roof onto the finals crowd (numbering about one hundred and fifty), I beat Ann Jones for the first time. It might not have been a major tournament, but for me it was a major breakthrough.

Developing with one star player ahead of you creates a definite bridge to gap. They're ahead of you, naturally enough, when you're very young, but that dominance seems to go on forever. They don't usually retire or abdicate when you want them to. The only answer is to beat them outright. I know exactly how Sue Barker must feel about me. She must think I've been in the number-one spot long enough. Although the age difference is greater than between Ann and me, the average length of time a player can go on is much longer now than it was.

Ten years ago, a woman was expected to reach her peak by twenty-five at the latest. I am so much better in every way now, including physically, that age obviously has become an arbitrary gauge. Modern ideas in training have helped sustain a greater flexibility preventing more injuries. As they become increasingly persuasive, the reasons to stay longer in the game cannot be ignored.

But more of that later.

Back to the amateur days. Before open tennis arrived, the game we played could hardly have been called a truly amateur sport. The sums we were paid for appearing at tournaments might seem negligible compared with our 1977 prize money, but for those days they were considerable.

All expenses were paid. Nearly everything you made was profit. Moreover, the tax man wasn't especially interested in your gains which were usually paid in cash. At the end of a tour some of the big stars would literally be carrying around bundles of different national currencies.

I wasn't a big star; just a young player more promising than most, with a knack for producing surprises on the tennis court.

Invitations to tournaments were abundant. The idea was to avoid the cold weather and follow the tour around the sunny side of the world. I could hardly wait to return to South Africa to see the trees, the long grass, the sea and the mountains, the wild openness and the familiar cities and friends I missed. South African patriotism had yielded to a British adoption. It took me five years to consider myself truly English, but once it happened it was final. All the same, my return was enveloped by a "home girl done good" attitude which encouraged me to try to win, especially in Durban.

On these trips we were treated exceptionally, housed by hosts "extraordinaire" and generally spoilt. In Cape Town, where my own abode had once been a dishevelled rectory, my host was none less than an Admiral of the Royal Navy. Arriving on the doorstep of the Admiralty House there was many a flutter of my heart as visions of Lord Nelson, the Duke of Edinburgh and brocaded striped uniforms raced through my mind.

I took several deep breaths and gathered my pile of racquets under my arm. I reminded myself that I was Virginia Wade (which didn't do much to reassure me) smiled a lot and walked in, instantly relieved by the welcome I received.

The week went by at breakneck speed. Where I found time to win the tournament I don't know. The once-in-a-lifetime experience of having sailors attend my every whim had to come to an end. I would have to return to the homely style of eating breakfast in the kitchen instead of in bed on a tray brought by a sailor.

Bloemfontein, a town in the middle of the baking hot hinterland, should surely have seemed the most dingy anti-climax. Yet, even there, a surprise awaited me. My Afrikaans hosts, both charming and hospitable, had a drive at the back of their house where there appeared to be a mass of garages. Inside were fifteen of the most stately vintage cars I'd ever seen; a Facel Vega, Bugatti, several Rolls-Royces and Bentleys, the oldest from 1904. I wonder whether those splendid cars are still there or perhaps have been appropriated by some Arab millionaire.

So these tournaments went. International stars being a rarity, the tennis was well attended. The local press was attentive and generous. I seemed to have acquired some consistency in my results although the competition was not quite the best. My next circuit proved to be more of a test.

I travelled with Ann Jones for eight weeks on the Caribbean tour, a circuit which for years had been raved about. Usually I preferred independence, befriending the local hosts and meeting people. The tournaments were mixed too, so there were plenty of male players to socialise with. But we were doubles partners so it seemed worth the sacrifice of some of my freedom. Pip, Ann's husband, a director of a paint factory, came over to visit later on so that let me off the hook for a while.

This tour was not for me.

The second week, in Jamaica, I lost early to a Dutch girl. Usually my losses are forgotten with the passing of time, however wretched they might have made me at the moment. This one remains. I was so disgusted with myself that Ann suggested if I really felt that miserable I should pack up and go home. Her suggestion had the opposite effect on me. There was no way I would return home vanquished. Instead I pulled myself together, went out on the practice court and made a resolution never to do so badly again.

I stuck out the circuit. We were all over the place. Venezuela, Columbia, Curacão, Mexico, etc. The travelling was painful with those outgrown inadequate airports. Each weekend we'd dread the sweaty heat in the ˌnon-airconditioned terminals, standing on an interminable line for an official who was bound to doubt the authenticity of your visa. Luggage was always overweight so we developed deft techniques of sticking our toes under the bags on the scales.

There were plenty of good moments, though.

Snorkeling amongst the multi-coloured tropical fish and sharks certainly beat playing at Queen's Club in the winter. Swimming and sailing at midnight under the brightest full moon was something only the Tropics could offer. And eating Spanish and local delicacies or exotic fruits made up for everything. In retrospect the discomforts were worth the experience of having gone. My best tennis was better than it had been. My worst was still bad.

The struggle of the Caribbean paid off at Bournemouth, 1967. In what I felt was my most intelligent match to that date, I beat Ann Jones in the finals 6–1, 10–8. It was the induction of my brain into my tennis. I wish it had come to stay.

It was Ann who did well in Rome and Paris and got to the final at Wimbledon that year, not me. At least I reached the quarters and consoled myself that it was my first full-time year. I calculated being in the semis the next year, the final after that and by 1969 or 70 to be the winner.

The best laid plans . . .

My results fluctuated like a yo-yo. There was always a story for the press who loved every see-sawing minute. There was scarcely a report that didn't mention the word "temperamental". Sometimes I had "ice-blue eyes", sometimes "blazing". Most commonly I was "tempestuous", "explosive", "unpredictable", "arrogant", "sultry", "scowling", "glowering".

We were paid appearance money so my results didn't affect me financially. The money didn't make any difference to me anyway. I hated the constant talk of it. It seemed right that open tennis should exist, even more so that the best players, both pros and amateurs, could play together at tournaments.

I had my feelings about turning pro. I was adamant that I shouldn't be a puppet of the professional promoter. The idea of playing one-night stands, being told when and where to play offended my sense of freedom. Tennis as a job, with a set routine with the same opponents didn't yet appeal to me. I wasn't sure I could push myself into good performances every night, not having arrived at the stage where pride in my performance was the strongest and only essential spur to playing well.

If the money was there, that was fine. If not, I wasn't going to go out of my way to procure it.

Four of the girls (Billie Jean, Rosie Casals, Ann Jones and Frankie Durr) turned professional in March, 1968. There was already a group of men pros. Without them the game was thin. Open tennis was the only solution.

The first open tournament materialised after a defiant struggle by the British Lawn Tennis Association. Not too many countries were in favour and threatened barring those players accepting prize money from their tournaments. Bournemouth, in April of 1968, was the site of the first Open with first-prize money of eight hundred pounds for the men and three hundred for the women.

I won, but—both because my status was uncertain and because the prize money so much lower than the men's—with my ice-blue eyes blazing, I arrogantly, gloweringly, scowlingly refused the money!

From the success of Bournemouth in April, 1968, I charted my course directly towards Wimbledon. The Wightman Cup was the first major grass event in advance of it. Every year before Wimbledon there are a few run-up tournaments where the players can get a chance to familiarise themselves with the grass surface.

In the mid-sixties, apart from major championships around the world, the Davis and Wightman Cups were the most prestigious international team events. Not only did I want to contribute towards a British victory, but I wanted to use the opportunity of playing on the Wimbledon courts as a preamble to the championships.

I started off like a bomb, annihilating Mary Ann Eisel 6–0, 6–1. Winnie Shaw and I won our doubles. These two were our team's only wins against the American's three with two matches left to be played.

My work had been plainly unfurled. I had to defeat

Nancy Richey or Great Britain was out. It was a prodigious responsibility, but I knew I'd be bolstered by a supportive team.

I won the first set 6–4. That effort temporarily drained me and we split sets. There was a ten-minute interval during which I braced up, remembering the feeling of the first set.

At 5–3 to me in the third set there came the bugbear of our contest two years before when I had 5–3 against her in the third and lost.

This time I won, to tie us 3–3 in matches.

In the final match of the series, a doubles, Christine and Nell Truman slithered and sprawled all over the dewy grass as darkness descended over the Number One court. The rest of the team sat grabbing and clutching at each other in giddy hysterics. If we won, it would be the first time in eight years the British had done so.

The end of the match was more like a surrealistic Monty Python skit than tennis doubles. Stephanie de Fina lacerated a serve that would have decollated Christine at the net if she hadn't dived to avoid it. Gales of nervous laughter from the crowd. The very next point Kathy Harter knocked a volley from close to the net straight in Christine's direction. Again she hit the ground. This time there were guffaws from the players as well.

Finally Nell lunged for a winning volley to give us the match.

At Merion, Philadelphia, with
Roger Taylor

A pause between games in a
Centre Court match against
Evonne Goolagong in 1973

Sharsted Court in Kent

The white cat is Simon, "British Hardcourt Champion, 1976"

Virginia and Bobby Charlton at their investiture in 1973, when Virginia was awarded the MBE

The Dewar Cup, 1969, Virginia with the Rt. Hon John Dewar and Lew Hoad (drinking)

In action during a Dewar Cup match

The Wightman Cup team, Deeside, 1974. *From left to right:* **Lesley Charles, Glynis Coles, Sue Barker, Sue Mappin, Virginia**

We were on the court before the four of them finished shaking hands. We had won the Wightman Cup! Instead of receiving the booby prize—the bouquet of red roses that filled the cup—as we had ever since I'd first played, we had finally won the trophy. The team was ecstatic. For a moment I felt sympathy for the Americans, knowing too well how it felt to be the loser, but that didn't last long.

The press talked about my rescuing the British team. "If anyone was responsible for winning, it was this sultry, sometimes scowling, sometimes emotional young woman. This was a performance as controlled, as disciplined, as intelligent as had ever been produced by this unpredictable player. Virginia played each ball as she saw it. For the first time Nancy was lured into making mistakes."

Praise it was, indeed. But how I longed to be rid of the temperamental trademark.

During the intervening week before Wimbledon my hopes ran high. The press maximised my chances. I was seeded No 5. My draw looked quite good. Ladbrokes quoted me at 12 to 1. (Better than this year—16 to 1.) I was Britain's brightest hope.

Wimbledon arrived. It rained for three and a half days. I had some crazy idea that the confusion of rushed practice on the wood at Queen's would be more detrimental than not practising at all.

At 7.30 on a Thursday night, I was put on court No Two against Christina Sandberg, a relatively unknown

Swedish girl whom I'd beaten comfortably before. After so many days off I was glad to play. That didn't last long. I felt as though I hadn't been on a court for weeks. With all that rain, it was more like a duck pond. As I skidded around in an ever-increasing spiral of bewilderment, Christina had merely to keep the ball in court to beat me.

What an embarrassing nightmare. This was the year my target was to reach the semifinal at least, and I was beaten in the first round.

I remember my brother Anthony discussing it with me afterwards at a forlorn gathering. "What you have to do," he said, "is start treating tennis as a regular job. When you don't feel like playing or things are against you, you still have to perform your job. Playing a match like that is like going into the office on Monday mornings."

It made sense in theory, but it clashed with the notion of doing well without slogging. Also, if I approached it in a vaguely dilettante way, sub-consciously that was still an excuse for imperfection.

My name might not have appeared at the end of the Championships in the role of victor, but I did win the Plate, the consolation event for first-round losers. It didn't console me much, but did help to at least redeem a little of my injured self-respect. Greater consolation came from the photos in the papers of "Virginia", a baby giraffe named after me. Making her debut at the London Zoo at two weeks old, she was said to be coming along nicely and already six foot ten inches tall.

My image was a source of great self-consciousness, yet the more I tried to hide all signs of aggravation, the harder it was to relax. I thought of quitting, reassessing the whole thing and starting over again if I felt like it. There was even doubt in my mind whether I should play the next big tournament, Forest Hills.

It was the first US Open Championships, with a large purse, but you had to win a few rounds to cover the airfare.

I wasn't used to fending for myself. Till then all my fares had been already covered. I was rather pessimistic about the whole event.

Forest Hills was always a struggle. The dressing rooms were over-crowded and uncomfortable. The courts were dreadful. All the European players referred to them as cow pastures. Fighting one's way out there on the subway in New York's sweltering August heat was a trial by fire before you even arrived at the club.

I considered opting out. Then that seemed rather a cowardly thing to do. I decided to play, with the emphasis not on winning, but on suffering emotionally as little as possible on court.

I knew I had to improve my concentration; also to resist getting mad with blind linesmen or any gamesmanship tactics.

On the other hand, the joy of playing abroad was

being isolated from the opinions, expectations, and judgments; in short, the pressures imposed by the British press. However diligently I tried to avoid reading newspaper reports in England, someone was sure to tell me exactly what was written, especially the gossipy stories. My outside shell was riddled with cracks where it had been weakened by the continual thrust of verbal jabs. It took me years to develop enough self-security to be able to follow my own judgment without being influenced by over-sensitive reactions to outside opinion.

At Forest Hills '68 this decision on approach dispelled temporarily the onus of my own expectations and confused psychological grip of the game. The usual obstacles disappeared. My serve troubled me briefly, but there was Doris Hart waiting to give me advice. It took ten minutes for her expertise to set me straight.

My draw was tough, but none of my opponents was a personal *bête noire*.

My first-round match against Stephanie de Fina had a few shaky moments. She was an astute player. Her left-handed lobs into the sun were very shrewd.

In the round of sixteens I had to play Rosie Casals. As we walked down the path to the stadium, she grumbled about the tournament, the early hour of the match, the balls, etc. For an instant I felt the old familiar feeling creep over me.

Then, as quickly as it came, I discarded it and

thought, "I'm feeling great. I'm looking forward to this match. Use it in your favour that Rosie likes to sleep late."

Rosie and I usually played close, exciting matches. Neither of us could resist the temptation to go for spectacular effects, nor had the slightest belief in half measures. If the audience could not be moved to wonder and applause, the game was hardly worth playing. This was a typical match. We both had successions of good points. Fortune fluctuated back and forth between us, but the composure and eagerness I felt before the match survived. I won 6–4, 7–5.

A sigh of relief issued from me. I'd covered my air fare from London and justified my No 6 seeding.

Next, I confronted Judy Tegart, probably the most exuberant of all the players. She'd been around for years, hovering near the top. We played a similar type of game only hers was more beefy and bouncy and less improvised than mine. I had a few more wins in our head-to-head record. She was at her peak though, having reached the final of Wimbledon earlier that summer. I expected a fight. Before I knew it, I'd won the match 6–2, 6–3. It was so easy; winner after winner streaming from my racquet. Only once had I winced at a bad bounce and then thought, "Shut up and get on with it." It was Judy who was literally tearing her hair out in despair at the turn of events.

I had reached the semifinal of Forest Hills and it hadn't even been difficult. The others had struggled

to reach their spots. Maria Bueno had beaten
Margaret Court, Ann Jones and Billie Jean had had no
easy route.

There was no problem getting geared up to play
Ann. We were constant rivals for the British top
ranking. While I was playing so well I was going to
make sure I did my best to beat her.

We were total opposites in style and temperament.
Ann was the shrewdest competitor in the women's
game; a realist, industrious, accurate, conscious of her
own powers and doing everything possible within
her limits. It was Head versus Heart; sophisticated
tennis versus natural ability.

I had beaten her in three out of the last four matches
we'd played, so it wasn't surprising that I did win the
semi, but the margin was, as the *New York Times* said,
"impressive". There was general astonishment that
my concentration never wavered, that I played such a
mature match at such a vital time. In 43 minutes it had
been neatly parcelled and packaged: 7–5, 6–1.

That evening I replayed every point of the match,
over an enormous dinner with David Gray, who was
then the tennis writer for the *Guardian*. David and I
frequently ate together. We were both equally crazy
about good food and sniffing out remote original-
type restaurants.

I talked incessantly but was positive about my
match the next day. "Now I've made it to the final,
I'd jolly well better win it!"

I slept well that night in my room at the Roosevelt Hotel. I didn't think too much about the tennis. In the morning I was raring to go. There were a few good luck telegrams from home and a call from Maureen Connolly. "Little Mo" had helped me more on my game than anybody else. She wished me luck and told me I could win it. That call meant a lot to me.

The day dragged on forever. The final between Billie Jean and myself was scheduled at five o'clock after the men's singles semifinal. I wanted to play that day; not to have to sustain concentration and anticipation another twenty-four hours longer.

I'd pick up a book, read a few pages without absorbing a thing, watch a few games, then start all over again. Finally Arthur Ashe beat Clark Graebner. It was closer to 5.30. Shadows were coming over the stadium court, but no one in the capacity crowd moved from his seat.

I didn't think about the match. It was my first really big final and for the first ten minutes I was trembling with nerves. Once they evaporated I was completely involved in the tennis. I loved every one of the forty-two minutes it took to beat Billie Jean. To me, my game seemed over-simplified, almost dull; percentage first serves, decisive but unflashy volleys. I kept expecting to have to produce more, but it wasn't necessary. I won 6–4, 6–2.

I was the first US Open Champion.

The end of the set always seems to signal the crowd to stretch their legs and exchange a few editorial observations with their neighbours. I think they forget it's not the same as a first-act intermission where the lights go up and to sit in your seat is the exception. Applause for the winner of the set fades away but the residual chatter and shuffling of feet goes on well into the opening point till they realise play is continuous. They're allowed a rest period. The rebound off those wooden benches isn't exactly spongy.

While they were up to that, for me it was a matter of strict business. My approach hadn't worked in the first set; the first chance was finished and there wasn't much leeway left. There was no alternative; I had to tighten my buckle and thievishly go after each point.

I gritted my teeth and tossed my head with emphasis. "Good . . . I like the way I feel now . . . just play . . . to hell with it being the final . . . you're out here to win two sets from someone . . . that's all . . . that's all you have to do . . . just play a match . . . what if you were playing her someplace else . . . " I remembered two matches I'd played against Betty in Atlanta and Palm Springs in the autumn of '76. I had been several match-points down and struggled back to win them both in the end. It was matches like those that would help win this one.

"This is a contest . . . compete . . . you're going to win . . . just Do it . . ."

My body finally felt my own; my racquet as if it were an extension of my arm. I wanted that first point in the second set more than anything. At the Royal Box end, I tossed the ball up. My serve flowed. It was smooth and too effective for Betty to return. Now I'd won that point, I wanted the next. The following two were identical. 40−0.

I was past the subconscious idea of wanting to play an immaculate match. As far as I was concerned all the matches before this had been perfect and I'd hoped to recreate another in the finals. At 5−4 it dawned on me that I was going for the final effect without starting from the first step and systematically progressing through each of the necessary preceding ones.

Once I'd realised that, each coming point counted as though the whole match depended on it. My mind had shifted into top gear; the mental immersion was total. All I needed was for my mechanical operations to catch up one hundred per cent. I was confident that would happen.

After all, that morning at 11.00 when I'd practised at Queen's, my timing and shot execution were first class. I'd never hit the ball better. There was no reason why three hours later they shouldn't be as good. The only environmental difference was that the court at Queen's had been flooded the day before and was softer than the Centre Court which took a little adjustment.

I miscalculated only one shot. At 40–15 I hit another good first serve which forced an error from Betty. It had been a definitive game; what I wanted. 1–0 to me. I strode to the side of the court feeling the contest was just beginning. I'd worked out my major problem. A minute isn't long at the change-over if your mind is unassembled, but when you're in control you feel you almost have time for afternoon tea.

It was all business as I glanced up and nodded at my friends in the stands. Each one playing on the Centre Court gets four tickets for the match in a special guest box. I saw Mr and Mrs Stove up there, too, probably feeling alone and outnumbered by all the partisan supporters. I hoped my guests weren't adding to their sense of exclusion. Tennis players' parents have a tacit code of behaviour to each other and to other players. None of the competitiveness shows up between them. They'd always been charming to me on the occasions we'd met. Apparently Mrs Stove is the anxious spectator and Mr Stove the more relaxed one. Just the opposite from my parents.

I sat quietly taking a drink. My mind was on the basic tennis essentials as I focussed and unfocussed on the grass by my feet. When the breather was over, I took a handful of sawdust from a box on the umpire's stand. I brushed it over my racquet handle to dry it off and improve the traction on the grip. I walked out, wanting to break serve immediately.

During a match there can be so many fluctuations of mood. For a stretch of several games you might feel as though nothing can stop you. Then you can practically see that sensation take flight and alight like a butterfly on your opponent's shoulder. It might happen through a mental lapse or some quirk of fate during a rally.

I can remember a match on the Centre Court where exactly that happened. I played Karen Krantzke in the first round. We were having a terrific struggle. I couldn't seem to keep the ball away from her fearsome forehand. She won the first set 8–6. At 1–1 in the second, I threw myself at a backhand volley and just got my racquet on it. The ball crawled over the net and died on her side. From then on, I didn't look back. The momentum had completely changed course on that one shot.

In this match against Betty I could feel the momentum turning. On Betty's serve I played a much better game. My shots were more solid and flowing. I went for them and immediately my anticipation improved.

I hit a forehand passing shot for a break and a 2–0 start. The sound of the hoorays was obvious above the applause. Things were going better. I didn't want to think too much about the next game; just keeping the errors down.

A wave was carrying me along, but it was like one of those secondary waves further out from the shore which can start off so promisingly and fade away in the general swell. If I kept my game neat and orderly and didn't try to be too clever, I could get enough distance out of it to take me where the big rollers were.

I served well and hit more good ground strokes than I had the entire match. My footwork was better too; nice compact quick steps instead of longer, less co-ordinated strides. On a tennis court, the short, quicker paces are the most efficacious. It's easier to arrive at the ball on the correct foot and make quick turns. That's why height is not always an advantage.

At 15 all, I hit a good smash off a tough lob. There was more than the usual response from the audience. That's another of the singularities of a tennis crowd. However mediocre an overhead might be, it is applauded with greater gusto than a tougher but subtler shot.

I suppose it's because the overhead seems such a formidable shot for the average club player to execute. It's quite easy. The trick is, the moment you see the lob coming up you have to turn your shoulder so that you're sideways to the net. Get your racquet right up and run back in little sideways steps like a crab; i.e., not directly backwards square on to the net. Then hit the ball slightly in front of you at full stretch. You should have the feeling of hitting down on the ball. It's easy, unless the lob is very good!

Anyway, I won that point. At 30–15 I served hard down the middle but missed by inches. My toss was slightly over my head to the left, making me go off balance. I did exactly the same on the second serve, but it went in a little short, which threw Betty a bit. She just missed the return and I won the game.

3–0 was certainly better than 2–1, but I still didn't have the reins tightly in my hands. I was acutely aware of this. I was trying to get hold of Betty's game with my own, but hers was like a slippery fish just reeled in from the water.

My win at Forest Hills was almost too good to be true. All I had wanted to do was get through it emotionally unscathed. Instead I'd hit a streak of good form and romped through all those players. My thrill at winning was tantamount to someone winning the football pools.

With my cheque for $6,000 I returned home triumphantly, surprised to see the splash I had made at home. Apparently, it was almost inconceivable that an English girl could actually win the US Open. The last one to do so was Betty Nuthall thirty-eight years before.

For days I was in demand. Photographers snapped me in every imaginable pose; with horses (I hadn't ridden in years), at the piano (hadn't played more than thirty minutes in the last twelve months), drinking champagne in the garden (from an empty bottle they'd supplied). It was all very heady stuff.

For a while I thought all this signified my permanent accession to the ranks of non-pareil. Gradually I realised I didn't know exactly how I'd won and therefore couldn't do it again at will.

My two years of full-time tennis were up. That was the period I'd counted on to gather a cluster of titles and exhaust my travelling urge. I'd done neither. I was nowhere near my tennis destination and globe trotting made a settled routine life seem humdrum.

I launched into the maelstrom of tournaments filled with a contraviety of feelings. My success in the second major event in the world revived my tarnished hopes for succeeding in other events, especially Wimbledon. If I'd won Forest Hills without actually having planned it, I could just as easily hope to hit a hot streak at Wimbledon. It had boosted my confidence in that respect. On the other hand, I now felt I had a reputation to live up to which was an albatross around my neck.

Before Forest Hills I had a date with myself for a referendum. If I failed the vote of confidence I would have to make a major reassessment. Winning the US Open only served to postpone the inevitable day of reckoning.

I maintain there are two approaches, at opposite ends of the spectrum, to playing the game. Either you can be totally relaxed about it; treat it as one of the casual happy-go-lucky activities of the day, never letting it interfere with your general disposition. You may come up with some great results precisely because of this nonchalance. Or, you can be utterly serious and professional about it; follow intricate plans, make sacrifices off the court, and put pressure on yourself to achieve certain goals.

This way you work in conjunction with a large element of tension. You require standards to be met so you worry lest you might fail. If you do win, you know you deserved it; if not, you did everything you could and cannot blame yourself.

The first group would say, "If I win, great; if I lose,

so what!" Perhaps someone like Evonne Goolagong could classify, with her enviable relaxed mental and physical demeanour; or, for that matter, anyone who plays more for the rewards of participation and recreation, than for the competition.

There's a story of Evonne once walking into the dressing room, where Chris Evert was shedding a few tears over a lost match. She took one look and disappeared. "I was so embarrassed" Evonne said later, "fancy crying over a tennis match!"

If you don't *naturally* fall into this category, there comes a moment when you realise that it just doesn't work for you. You *do* care about winning. You can *not* lose and come off saying, "Oh well, too bad!" This is when you discover instinct alone cannot sustain you. Improvisation isn't sufficient. You need mental technique.

There is no possibility that I could organically belong to this genre. Psychologically I'm just not made that way. But, in the early years as a full-time tennis player, this is just what I was trying to do. However hard I tried to be casual, it was in vain; losses maddened me. It was like fitting a square peg into a round hole. I *was* very competitive. I *did* care if I didn't win.

At the back of my mind I knew that one had to put in the effort to pull oneself out of a slump. At fourteen, I hated Latin at school and spent a minimum of time conjugating and declining words, translating extinct writings. In the end, my luck ran out and I flunked an exam. I went straight home and worked overtime. A month later, for one glorious moment, I came top of the class. I actually quite enjoyed it while my head was above water (the Rubicon), but I didn't relish Caesar's exploits enough to keep up that sort of effort. I returned to my more comfortable milieu of equations and left the book-worms to Hannibal.

There were two legitimate obstacles to my tennis progress. One was the scarcity of good coaches. I could find momentary guidance; a pearl of wisdom from Segura, a tip from Doris Hart, but there was no one to call on at the spur of the moment. The relationship between coach and player is very intricate and complex. There must be mutual respect and intellectual compatibility. Your success must matter as much to the coach as it does to you. The only relationships that really function are those where the player has started off as a protégé and grown up with the pro.

At the end of close matches which I'd lost, I'd think, "Why didn't I win that match?" I felt stranded; I didn't know what tactical or technical improvements to make.

There was one period of exception. Maureen Connolly had been appointed to coach our team during my first Wightman Cup match. From the minute I stepped on court with her I could see what made her so great. It wasn't just her reputation that I

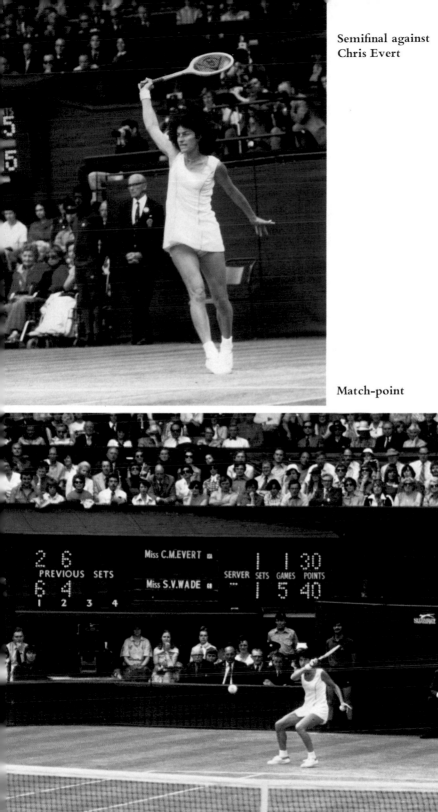

Semifinal against
Chris Evert

Match-point

Wimbledon 1977

respected. Her strength showed everything. There was more energy and positive wherewithal in those five foot two inches than I'd ever encountered.

On court, I responded to her guidance like a charm. I had so much esteem for her I put out all my concentration and effort, in an attempt to please her and do well.

I managed later to visit her a couple of times in Dallas, where she lived. By then she was seriously ill and suffering from the effects of cobalt treatments. She still insisted on coming out on court with me. When she was too ill to play, she'd arrange a partner, and coach from the sidelines. Her courage, at the end of her life, was as remarkable as it was at the beginning.

At her first Wimbledon, she had been forbidden to play by her coach because of bursitis in her shoulder. Maureen, refusing to accept the judgment, was immediately dropped by the coach. At seventeen, this might have seemed too heavy a blow, but Maureen proceeded to win her way through the entire tournament, on her own.

She never talked too much about her career. It was like a mission she had been obliged to accomplish, not a labour of love. Her three replicas of the Wimbledon salver were modestly displayed in her living room, but she didn't have time for remini-

Left: **triumph at last.**

scences. She was an absolute dweller in the present, always active and always thinking ahead.

She died the Saturday night before Wimbledon in 1969. I wished to make a tribute to her by winning the tournament. I didn't win, but Ann did. Ann too was a devoted friend of Maureen's. I often wondered whether the extra will to win came as a token of dedication.

The other hurdle facing a neophyte on the full-time tennis circuit was the rigour of travelling. To someone stuck in a nine-to-five rut, it might seem glamorous, away from the drudgery of daily life and homely chores; yet, those people probably would find even a small dose an overdose.

They'd start out like the seasoned traveller but after one month on the tennis circuit, the truth would come out. "It was evaso nice . . . Lovely sunshine . . . A little 'ot though if you ask me . . . Don't like quite sa much 'eat meself . . . Nothing like 'ome is there, luv? . . . You know, I'm dying' for a cuppa tea . . . 'ad to drink that filthy coffee . . . And the food, ya know . . . Don't care for all that foreign cooking meself . . . First thing I cooked when we got back was bangers and mash and baked beans . . . Wouldn't like to live abroad . . . It's such a relief to 'ear English again!"

Well, I didn't feel quite like that. I liked being assimilated into the local purlieus. Probably my favourite time was mingling with the native residents during their Sunday promenading; on the Palatine Hill in Rome; around the street stalls in South America; in the parks in Paris. Sunday can be so flat at home, yet away it comes to life with the gentle pulse of a Brueghel scene.

One's visit abroad is a success when people don't look at you and know right away you're a foreigner. For me the height of being a non-tourist is to be able to negotiate my way around on the local buses or subways. Moscow was an exception though, where it was impossible to decipher a station's name in the Cyrillic alphabet. In Greece, I was a little more adept at scrambling into the rickety old buses. I enjoyed being huddled in with black-shawled women cross- ing themselves, and angry hens clucking at every ikon we passed.

It may all sound very attractive and some of it was. But the reality of it week after week left the vacational aspect far behind. It reached the extent of laborious living out of a suitcase. Jet lag was routine. Packing was no longer a neat, scientific art. My clothes got so monotonous I was ready to donate them to the Salvation Army.

The hardest thing of all was to forecast months in advance how many tournaments in a row I'd be capable of playing. Looked at in the long term, capacity could stretch to encompass anything. When the time arrived, the limitations of bodily and mental fatigue suddenly surfaced.

I persevered, through some good patches and some horrible, until finally in the late summer of 1970 I hit rock bottom. My last match of the season was against Rosie Casals in the semi at Forest Hills. Each minute was agonising, but by habit I stayed there in body, if not in spirit. At the beginning of the final set there was a bad call, and an almost simultaneous muscle spasm in my back. I lost without any further trouble.

Like a clarion call, the facts rang clearly. My back only became strained when I was in a predicament. Obviously, it was because my muscles were tensed up and more injury-prone; even more, it provided me with a legitimate excuse for failure. Once I discovered that in myself, I didn't have to look far to find it happening all over the place—players getting cramp at match-point, or pulling a muscle when in a tight spot.

In addition, I had the revelation that somewhere in my nether being there was a fear of winning. I didn't seem to *want* to win. I was afraid of having to live up to a required standard and of the emptiness that had sometimes followed my successes.

These characteristics were apparent everywhere one looked. I had no admiration for them in others. When I discovered them in myself, it was obvious that I would have to learn how to relax. I couldn't go on any longer hating playing. It was against the very essence of my love for tennis. I'd either have to start enjoying my matches or quit.

For a month I escaped the circuit and the groove of home. I went to Greece, feeling that a new environment amongst friends would help rid me of bad habits. I came out refreshed and with a new leaf turned over. Each match I reminded myself to smile and have fun.

Rome was my favourite tournament. After all, it was the city I loved most. Playing in the Foro Italico, lined with marble statues and umbrella pines, one felt more like a gladiator than a tennis player. In 1971 I became the Italian champion.

It was a title I had dearly wished to win. The slowest, red clay courts in Europe, that had had the better of me for so long, were mastered. Patience and strategy had finally become part of my repertoire.

My newly-found relaxation was beginning to pay off. 1971 seemed as though it would be the year I'd come into my own. Except I had a couple of accidents that made it evident to me what the difference between real and imagined injuries was. Right after Rome I slipped and fell heavily on my wrist, resuming play and winning my semifinal against Rosie Casals, but being too hurt to play for weeks afterwards.

Then the week before Forest Hills I was playing Winnie Shaw in Orange, New Jersey. There had been flooding in the area so we were moved from the grass courts indoors. I'd lost the first set, won the second and was just getting into my stride, when I impetuously ran down a ball that I was unlikely to reach. I tried to enhance my chances by sliding the last yard. Alas, this wasn't grass—this was a surface with a high degree of traction, and my foot slid but my shoe remained firmly adhered to the floor.

The result was a sprained ankle that ballooned in front of my eyes, while I lay helplessly on the ground. Soon I was surrounded, feeling more foolish than ever, when Pierre Barthes, the beautiful Frenchman, came over, removing his jacket. "Let me pick you up and carry you inside," he said.

Just as I was reaching up to clasp him around the neck, thinking, "Gee, this isn't so bad", the policeman who was on duty said sternly, "Don't touch her. Don't move her."

He looked awfully fierce with his cowboy stance and his gun in his holster, so I slumped back on the floor obediently and waited to be carried off in an ambulance with flashing lights and clanging bells.

Observing the drama close by was Lance Tingay, the reporter of the *Daily Telegraph*. "I knew they shot injured racehorses," he was heard to say, watching the policeman stride out to the scene, "but I didn't know they shot injured tennis players."

The ankle healed. I started 1972 by winning the Australian Open title. My ambitions were not overly high; I was still healing all the scars of the past and layer by layer removing the integument of my temperamental image, but I never had another psychosomatic backache (any real problems now are solved by the

magical hands of Mr John Wernham, my osteopath),
and for the next couple of years I can honestly say that
I enjoyed every moment on court.

*Betty had won the first set; a sizeable accomplishment
considering her path was set with thorns. Temporarily
lulled, she fell behind. At 3–0, on a streak of games to me,
she woke from her reverie to the noise of fifteen thousand
people yelling. There was no decision to make. What faced
her was, obviously, on the wall. Either she caught up right
away or risked losing her one set lead.*

*She met that proposition, winning three of the last four
games she would for the rest of the match.*

*In a common spirit of devotion and enthusiasm the fans
had waited patiently through the first hour. They'd never
pressurised me or tried to force themselves on me. It was
almost like being told, in a gesture of undemanding soli-
darity, "We're here. Call if you need us." They never came
in uninvited. My run of three games had ignited them. Still
they waited obediently to be invoked.*

*At three all, there was a portentous lull before the blitz. I
walked behind the baseline at the Royal Box end, rested my
forehead in my right hand; a deceptively tranquil pose for
the foray about to follow.*

It was quiet. But for an occasional gust of wind rustling the backstop behind me, it could have been a film still. They were watching me stop—"Be still . . . think . . . listen . . ." I knew in the very centre of myself that I had something to rely on, to trust. There was a strong, reliable foundation. I expected to be here. I planned it. I deserved it. It was no hot streak. I had more to draw forth and draw from.

They watched me. Like two people who know each other very well, the Centre Court crowd and I share unspoken thoughts. We're mutually reciprocal. They had given me their support. Right now I gave them my conviction.

No one can deny that having fifteen thousand people standing shoulder to shoulder with you isn't a big help. But they'd been rooting for me the year I lost to Christina Sandberg in the first round, the year I lost to Pat Walkden in the third round, the year of defeat by Ceci Martinez in the fourth round. They couldn't help then. They'd only been infected with the contagion of my hysteria. They could only help if they knew I could help myself.

Maybe for an instant there was the image of a defeated Virginia, but it was just a vision the scoreboard suggested. If I'd won the first set 6–0 and led 5–1 in the second, it wouldn't have entered anyone's mind. I'd lost the first 6–4 and it was 3–3 in the second. But I do not think, as they studied me collecting thrust, that anyone did really, with any seriousness, entertain the thought that I could fail. No one accepted my losing as a realistic possibility; not here, this day, this year. It wouldn't mesh.

They were quiet in their faith. Though they couldn't

The New York "Apples" team.
Standing left to right: **Virginia, Sandy Mayer, Billie Jean King, Fred Stolle (Coach); kneeling, Linda Siegelman, Ray Ruffles, Lindsay Beaver**

After a hard-played doubles match with Evonne Goolagong in Dallas, Texas

A rare "behind the camera"
shot at Eastbourne

Sightseeing in Hong Kong

come on court bodily to help, they conducted their will, strength and power through the lightning rod of my corporeality with each palm-stinging clap, every nail-bending, clenched fist, through the sound of every sibilant energising "Yes" they whispered to convince me.

I belonged to them; their creation, and they had pulled the lever to animate me.

I took the new balls and showed them to Betty in the customary gesture without taking my eyes off the ground or breaking the thread of courage. It was as though I were standing on the top diving board knowing that I'd performed a complicated dive a thousand times, but was still holding my breath for that instant of suspense.

Almost on the same breath I served, deep into her backhand; I was close in to the net behind it with a new gust of wind in my sails. My backhand volley was decisive, setting me up for another, a forehand volley. I saw it coming. I stretched to my right and hit it sweetly off the middle of the racquet. Betty couldn't do anything. Slowly, I walked back to the baseline feeling the rhythm of well-oiled co-ordination coming over me. I served and stayed back, pounced on the opportunity to get to the net with a backhand approach shot. I judged it exactly; taking the ball with me as I sped to the net. She was forced behind the baseline. Instinctively, a drop volley just glided off my racquet. I didn't think about it. My reflexes and subconscious brain were with me now.

I was neither congratulating myself nor driving myself on; just being what I had spent so many hours calculating to be. *The next serve was an ace, my first of the match, bringing up a cloud of chalk on the sideline. I rocked on the baseline for my next serve. It hit the top of the net. I noticed the ballboy swiftly gather it up; a passer-by as in a dream. The second serve was deep into the box. I knew what to do with the approach shot. It was my game for 4–3.*

I had entered the trance-like, almost hypnotic state. It's one of the gear stages that absolute involvement in a match brings. It can last for some time; never for a whole match, but while in it, you try to get as much mileage as possible.

We changed ends. I sat like a somnambulist, blanking my mind out, just staring at the blades of grass. When we left our chairs, my body was relaxed but functioning like a cat on the run. I didn't have to prompt it into action. It was working involuntarily.

She served a little deep so I had to return anyway. It screamed off my racquet; a winner. I smothered a Cheshire Cat smile.

My backhand connected with her second serve; she hit a volley, long. There was a query on the call. I hardly noticed the disruption. It didn't matter what decision the officials made.

In the next few points I played a whole string of winning forehands. They felt great. I'd gallop to the ball and line it up. The ball would get bigger and bigger and seem to stop in mid air to be devoured. I aimed and fired.

I was 5–3 up, feeling better every minute. The clapping and cheering swelled over the stadium as I hit the crowd's favourite, a clean winner. They could see it coming and played it from their seats, clapping almost before it landed.

We were ready for the next game before the noise had simmered down. It's a great compliment, being forced to wait for the applause to abate after you've won a point. The umpire requested quiet. Instantly there was a hush. In the cathedral silence, I suddenly became aware of each movement I was making. I wondered whether my grip on the handle was the same I'd been using all the time, whether that slight shuffling of my back foot to get balanced before the serve was new. An eternity seemed to pass in a flash. The last thing I wanted to do was rush, but, oh, that silence —all those eyes pinned on me.

I reminded myself of a conversation I had with Ken Fletcher the night before I played Chris. "You know what to do Virginia, but just remember if you get tense, keep going for your shots with more spin and camp out at the net."

I threw the ball up to serve; it just missed but it felt like any other serve; the little amount of discomfort was over.

I served an ace to line myself up with two set points. At 40–15 I went for a big serve down the middle. The crowd cheered and clapped. They had to laugh at themselves. I smiled briefly, knowing that I, too, had hoped it was in. Betty shook her head at them. With all those people pulling against her, I couldn't blame her. She won that point with a fine backhand volley.

Another chance. The serve hit the spot I wanted. I got a short return to come in on and slid my backhand onto her baseline; she made a classic lob deep and high over my right shoulder. I scooted back, climbed right up in the air for it, extended from one extremity to the other and crunched it. I couldn't have asked for a better point on which to win a set.

I have literally been through two tennis lives. The first was the instinctive spontaneous approach to the game. With it I'd won the titles of Forest Hills, Rome and Australia. The second life of today is the much more intellectual and professional one. I've learned that it's not enough to do something well. You have to know *how* you did it to be fully satisfied and to ever expect to recreate it. Being good isn't good enough. You have to know why and how; you have to submit to technique.

For years I had no real direction. I found myself dredging barren reserves to overcome problems I couldn't even identify. Through the chaos I looked for the awareness of myself and surroundings, that would finally translate into terms of my tennis career.

Gradually the search spawned a clearer understanding of personal objectives. The last year I played Wimbledon without these additional new perceptions was 1974 when I lost to Olga Morozova in the semifinal.

1975 was the first year I had no doubt that I was good enough to be the Wimbledon champion. I'd beaten all the top players during the year; my tennis had been more masterly than ever. The unpredictability had been virtually eradicated. That season during Team Tennis I'd worked slavishly with Fred Stolle, Billie Jean and the team. At Eastbourne, the tournament leading up to Wimbledon, I defeated Martina Navratilova in the semi and Billie Jean in the final, so that I was assured my current form was top notch.

I was optimistic. In the closing minutes before I went on court to play Evonne Goolagong in the quarterfinal of Wimbledon, I summarised my objectives. I wanted to be certain when I came off court that I had done everything in my power to win; not be allowed to say, "If only I'd done this instead of that I might have won."

We played a match of the most superlative calibre. It was as though a master mind were computing each play and counter-play for the ultimate in precision.

I came within two points of winning what was later voted the best match of the tournament. Reconciling myself to that loss when I'd played so well was nearly impossible. All the sporting palaver about somebody having to lose only made it worse. I didn't see why it had to be me. It was, as all close matches are, just a matter of a few points.

Someone said to me later, "Don't try to interpret or understand it. It doesn't make sense to you now; it may never, but there's a reason. Hopefully, it may be apparent to you sometime. Right now you have to accept the confusion as a challenge. You've actually been given a gift in the form of this lesson. If you face the challenge, you can exercise your will and strengthen it for future use."

It all made so much sense, and if nothing else, at the moment, the idea of a different, more tangible challenge comforted me. There was a choice how to react. I could sulk or I could use the defeat to edify myself. I wasn't going to be defeated twice in one day.

In a spiritual context, dealing with that quarterfinal loss as an imponderable beyond my explanation, made sense. But I wanted to fit it into a day to day context; make it something I could use to help myself. I construed it this way: I had not come through a really tough quarterfinal because I had never constructed a final destination for myself. If I had firmly believed that I had to be in the final and win the tournament, then there would have been a lot less chance of losing in the quarterfinal. Let's say I had six out of eight cylinders firing. You can get an incredibly long way without that last ounce, but it is essential as the winning factor; also the hardest·to put in.

It was at this point that I made the decision. I would have to change.

If I were to have any realistic hope of winning Wimbledon I had to begin to *want* to. It wouldn't just happen. That wasn't for me. I would plan it. I would expect it. It would become the goal to think about every day. It would give my tennis a sense of direction. There's a big difference between passively *wishing* and actively *wanting*. If you waste time wishing you avoid using practical solutions to attain the goal.

I began to see myself as an individual personality not responsible for the expectations of others. What I had to do was correct my technical weaknesses and leave the press and public to sort out their image of me in whatever way they liked.

I'd always been looking for the answers, but glossed over really the most basic ones. I wouldn't dream of skipping on court practice, but I'd casually omitted "skull practice"; creating difficult situations on court and figuring out the best way of dealing with them, so that when they really did come up they weren't disruptive.

Now I'd be able to experience uninterrupted concentration. I could make the choice of how to react to a potential distraction. A crisis can bring strength and power or rob one of the usual level of control and skill. I began to realise, with my new goal uppermost in mind, that to indulge a mental lapse would not contribute in any way to my aim.

Practice sessions became not only hitting the ball in various drills but rehearsing the mentality I would have to recreate during a match. This was the security of mental technique; creating calmness and clarity of thought which could be trusted to carry over in a real crisis situation. I was now doing something that for years I had dreaded would adulterate my spontaneity. I was combining pure instinct with an intellectual process; the extemporaneous with thought, calculation. Once I became inured to the process I had to admit that the combination was a truer art form than either component could be separately. Now it was simple; religious training equalled irreproachable mental and physical technique equalled the freedom to be creative and spontaneous.

It's difficult for most people to imagine the creative process in tennis. Seemingly it's just an athletic matter of hitting the ball consistently well within the boundaries of the court. That analysis is just as specious as thinking that the difficulty in portraying King Lear on stage is learning all the lines.

People have said to me, "How can you hit so many backhands in a row without missing?" That's the same as asking the actor how he can remember all the words. They're the least important part of his performance. The first thing he has to do is get the words out of the way. On stage, his concentration is no longer on stringing them together or picking up his cues. He's worked out what the lines *mean* and created his subtext to the point where the words have become second nature. Now he is free to create and spontaneously react to what is happening on stage. With the art of hiding the technique comes the illusion that the words are his own and are being spoken for the first time.

During a tennis match you can't think how to hit a backhand every time you get one. Nor can you wonder what your incentives and objectives are on a tough point. It's the homework, the creative process which you take out on the court with you. The more thoroughly it's done the less apt you are to give in during a contest of wills. The rehearsal has been done. You don't think about it during the match. You trust it and go out onto the court with infinite possibilities.

You can be alert enough, with this as your foundation, to find new ways on court to change a strategy, correct mistakes or generally respond to the feedback of the opponent.

It's what separates great players from good players; any brilliant performer from an adequate one.

Of course, because each individual brings his own life experiences to everything he does, addressing the task becomes a very subjective process. What one player uses for an incentive may be meaningless for the next. All the top players do have the very strong driving force in common, but beyond that their paths diverge.

How have players like Margaret Court, Billie Jean King, Chris Evert, Maria Bueno produced such formidable records?

Margaret won with imposing regularity. She so

adamantly refused to quit, even when she was looking down the barrel of a gun, that I used to wonder whether a loss for her was the total embodiment of failure. With Billie Jean it's not so much the loss that she is avoiding as the win she wants.

Margaret's record was gargantuan. On court, with the combination of her strength and indefatigable attitude, she was like a bull mastiff in the same cage with a white mouse. The outcome wouldn't depend on the other player's level of brilliance that day. You could be playing your best, she could be slightly off, but somehow, however close to the precipice she came, she seldom fell off.

I watched so many of her matches, or played in them, when there would be a crisis point. If she survived it, she'd be sailing free the rest of the match. She put all her money into this one vital point with the assurance of someone flipping a two-headed coin.

I remember playing her in the semifinal of Forest Hills in 1969, on a court squelching with rain. Neither of us was great, we were very even. I led 5–4 and 40–0 on her serve. She came up with a series of points that totally ignored my presence on the other side of the net. From then on she never put a foot wrong and I was wiped out.

Her performances were of a predictably indomitable level. She would always say, "Two hours a day isn't very long to concentrate."

I always felt that her incentive, as a very devout

Christian, was not to squander the gifts for which she felt God had selected her.

As for Billie Jean, there is no such uniformity of mood. Her plethora of victories comes from an equally strong driving force, but one of a very different nature. She *needs* to win. She loves to be driving herself in an atmosphere of intensity. As soon as one win is under her belt, she is looking forward to the next.

Dr Ogilvie, from San José, California, has drawn some conclusions from his study of 293 competitive athletes in risk-taking behaviour. I don't know if tennis can be considered "risk taking" in the context of his survey, which included acrobatic pilots, racing drivers, parachutists and fencers, but I still think some of his observations are applicable to Billie Jean.

"... these athletes are 'stimulus addicts'. The need to extend oneself to the absolute physical and emotional limits is the quest to escape from the bland, tensionless feelings associated with everyday living ... These men and women experience little joy in life when their true ability remains uncontested. They much prefer to have the odds against them because they find it impossible to invest their egos in pursuits that do not require the best they have to offer."

Billie Jean's behaviour seems to be concomitant with these suggestions. She's permanently fascinated by the game. Day after day in Team Tennis, she's experimenting with different shots or playing around with ideas at the drawing-board stage.

She seems to have as much fun psyching herself up as playing the match. In the New York Apples' dressing room, before a match, it's not uncommon to find one of Billie Jean's pep rally performances going on: "We gotta kill 'em tonight. We gotta kill 'em!! We're gonna be great!" In between exhortations she looks in the mirror and sings eight bars of "Say a Little Prayer for Me". "Thoose little boogers! I can't STAND losing to them!"

She puts on a Team Tennis uniform which has shrunk from too hot a drier. There's a shocked silence. "Geez Louise, look at this! Teddy would have a blue fit. I can't stand my dresses looking like tee shirts . . . I don't care any more. I just don't care. As long as we get on court and win. We gotta win 6–0!" She pulls a face into the mirror and shakes a fist at the reflection.

Billie Jean's always striving for an improvement. She's never content with a straight win. She'll find some instances in a match after she comes off that weren't up to her standards of perfection and set herself out to correct them. To keep herself constantly mentally alert she'll fabricate situations. Never at rest, she's always in a state of campaigning.

Chris Evert is yet another type of winner. She

enters a cocoon the moment she goes on court. It's as though she flicks on a switch and automatically she is in a frame of reference where all that matters is her apparatus working at precision efficiency. Day after day she produces infallible tennis. I imagine her total faith in the accuracy of her shots, the life-long training that her father instilled in her, and her habitual winning record give her sufficient confidence not to have to appeal to her reserves of psychological energy.

She plays with the same clinical approach against lesser and greater opponents alike. The excellence of her tennis alone, and the self-assurance that she belongs in the top niche, serve to ensure that she doesn't fall beneath.

I remember the Wightman Cup being played in Cleveland in August, 1971, with Chris making her first national appearance as a phenomenal sixteen-year-old. I'd never played her before.

The court was a synthetic rubber carpet laid on cement outside. When it was cool, it was slow. When the summer heat developed in the middle of the day the balls bounced like silly putty. There'd been a deluge of rain the night before and most of it remained in puddles under the carpet. If a ball hit one it produced a dull thud.

The score was heavily in Chris's favour as she hit winner after winner past me. When I'd had just about enough of these non-bouncing balls, in disgust I stuck my toe under the seam of the court. To my surprise it lifted up like a mat and revealed a sub-surface lake. Aha! I gleefully stooped down to see how far I could raise the court. Ann Jones, who was our captain came running over. "Virginia, don't do that! The court people are having a fit. They don't know how to fix it if it comes up. They're frantic."

Reluctantly I resumed the match. For Chris it had never been interrupted; monolithic concentration sustaining her while the rug had almost been pulled from under.

Maria Bueno was probably the player with the most presence and grace on the court. Where again did her incentives come from? She came from a well-off background; she wasn't brought up with tennis as a staple of the family diet; she did not have to prove herself on court for the sake of her general well being. I think she wanted to win because she just enjoyed the roll of the queenly prima donna.

She was a heroine in Brazil. Two statues stand in her honour in São Paolo. If her subjects wished to send a letter they could do so with a postage stamp bearing her image. She knew she was the most dazzling and most demanded player; that people would willingly kneel to kiss her ring. She knew exactly what she could command and did, but when her reign ended she had the innate dignity and grace not to demand attention as part of her pension right. For that she's been a perennial and sentimental favourite of any fortunate audience for whom she still occasionally performs.

As for me, I had been lucky enough to discover in ample time, a purpose in life that I excelled in. I didn't want to waste the golden opportunity to bring this natural endowment to fruition.

I'd developed higher expectations of myself and a pride in performing to that level. If I misused the chance, the regret would have perpetually plagued me.

I wanted to take the risk of change.

There's always a fundamental safety in being able to say, "That's the way I am," or, "That's the way it's always been"—with the implication that that's the way it's going to stay. It takes enormous effort and singlemindedness to effect a change in something so profound as your basic self. I was now willing to make a few mistakes and suffer a little for what I wanted.

I think most situations are within one's power to shape, depending on the efficacy of your choice. In this case, if I were to do everything in my power to attain the goal and not temporise by wishing, then I must face the changes and the unsettling interim period when I would have neither my old shots nor my new ones.

With the help of Jerry Teeguarden, whom I'd met years ago when he was coaching Margaret Court,

I changed parts of my game which had kept me among the top five women players in the world for years. My serve, for instance, had been dubbed "the best serve in women's tennis"; it wasn't up to the compliment. I was expending a tremendous amount of energy with less than satisfactory returns. I had almost to start from the beginning again to resurrect a serve that was more technically correct and that suited me.

If a person sets a goal not ludicrously beyond his limitations and works uncompromisingly to attain it, there is no way he can fail. I've never seen a person fail who can honestly say he's done the limit.

In the last few years I've learned that before and during a match if I create for myself the right climate of concentration, guts and determination and spend each minute doing everything I can to win, then I've gone the limit. That is the objective.

If I can do that, I win. If I don't, then I must be prepared when I come off the court to admit, "I didn't do everything I could. That's why I lost."

Before, I'd go through an apocryphal routine about bad calls, poor bounces, the lot. What I was actually doing was looking for an excuse; just *wishing* I'd win. Now if I want it I commit myself to the work involved in getting it, and the prospect of losing isn't nearly as scary.

No matter what your field, if you are dependent on luck for results, you're frightened. You've put

"How could I have missed that one?"

One dram too many . . .

Before the Final, with Ceddy, the stray black cat

yourself at the mercy of a force you can't possibly control. When you exert your own control, you're actively part of the situation, taking charge, no longer dependent.

That was what made this Wimbledon different from all the others. I knew I would be in the final. I had *planned* it.

At one set all, I had no intentions of changing my plans . . .

They had been like third-formers counting the minutes for final term bell. Now that it had rung, the fans thrashed the air with Unior Jacks and erupted in a burst of spontaneous combustion.

As I walked back to my chair a smile spread over my face. Even the photographers, the nearest members of the audience to me, were clapping while their cameras hung in wait for the next dramatic moment.

My eyes were caught by some of the closest spectators. They had fixed their gaze on me with the magnetic penetration that can even wake one from sleep. Their steady look drew me; nationalistic pride beamed from their faces.

The smile on my face didn't stay long; I was engulfed by a predatory desire for the next game. The applause tapered off and was replaced by the hum of discussion and laughter. The knowledge that they would be happily absorbed for the next sixty seconds in their own commentary, faded the hubbub into the periphery of my consciousness.

I sat awaiting my cue. It was like the times I'd shot television commercials; sitting there in between takes trying to keep the mood of the last reading so that when I heard, "We have sound . . . camera rolling . . . and action . . ." I'd be ready with the performance I'd done perfectly in my mind. Today I'd have the magic take when the assistant director "clapped the sticks" as they say to identify the next scene: "Virginia Wade, Wimbledon, 1977, take 16."

As we walked out to our respective ends, the crowd left their reflections at once to return and buoy us up. After seeing that advertisement of the Union Jack and "We're backing Britain" for so many years, one could see how well the feeling had been inculcated in them.

I flexed my legs to stretch them. After my match with Chris two days before, I had been quite stiff from sheer effort and exertion. Even today it had taken a set to loosen up completely. Now I was warm; all the remaining kinks ironed out.

Betty served; more accurately than she had been, but with a touch less force. I was putting extra pace on the ball, covering more ground; picking up shots which earlier had been winners and returning them with interest. More importantly, I wasn't making any errors.

I broke Betty's opening serve to be 1–0 up.

The crowd relaxed visibly. Theoretically, all I had to do

*now was hold my serve. For the first time in the afternoon I
was leading. I asked the ballboy for some orange juice and
allowed myself the luxury of predicting the shape of the last
set.*

I'm not a great believer in superstition, but I do share
with most everyone that pretty common curiosity for
crystal gazing. If there's a good omen, I'm more than
willing to accept it; if it's something I don't want to
hear, it's out. Through the last months of my quest
for the Wimbledon title there had been certain
serendipitous signs impossible to ignore. They'd
registered on my awareness one by one; like the final
pieces of a jigsaw puzzle, they were fitting into place
this afternoon to form a picture of me holding the
Wimbledon trophy high above my head.

In April, sixteen of us were en route from New
York to Tokyo to play in the Bridgestone Doubles
Championships. To pass the time, Virginia Ruzici,
one of the talented young Romanian players, was
employed to tell fortunes.

As we watched Vergie's long thin fingers shuffle the
cards, the Jumbo Jet lost its oriental influence and took
on the aspect of a gypsy encampment on the outskirts
of the Moldavian slopes.

Virginia's voice, which ordinarily has a graceful
rhythmic intonation had even more the cadence of a

prescient gypsy. All that was missing was the strolling gold-toothed violinist lost in his passionate music, immune to the hardships of the world.

Virginia sat in a middle seat; faces peering from over her shoulder and the seats in front of her. She dealt the cards onto the 747 tray-top table, hardly a likely surface for the prophetic faces of an oracular deck.

Her forecasts were amazingly accurate. The absent friends, the dark-haired visitors, the state of the girls' love lives all fell astonishingly into place.

My turn came. I recognised all the characters. At the end of our respective sessions, we were each given one last private wish. Vergie said, "Let's do this last one. If the cards fall right, your wish is granted. If they don't, it isn't. It practically never comes out, so don't expect much . . ."

The cards had been dealt around to all the girls; Frankie Durr, Janet Newberry, Billie Jean, Brigitte Cuypers and others. They all came up negative. I don't know what their unfulfilled wishes were, but I do know what mine was, and it was the only one to come up true . . .

I looked at the orange lying on the grass by my chair. There was a twinge of emptiness in my stomach, but I decided not to eat it during that change-over. I'd have to sticky my fingers peeling it or ask the ballboy to do it for me. The sound of my own voice catching his attention might snap the suspended state I was in.

It was nearly four hours since I had eaten, or rather, picked at my food. I'd sat up in the competitors' buffet trying to force food down, but my gullet was locked shut.

Earlier, at lunch I'd sat near the window and stared at the empty Number Two court. The results board right near it was blank except for Betty's and my name in the Centre Court slot and the junior's final on the Number One court.

Before matches I have to be reasonably replete. I continually seem to be starving on court, providing conjecture amongst the regular spectators as to what I'll eat next. It's usually only an orange or soft drink or chocolate or Dextrosol glucose tablets, but if I don't, I feel my stomach knocking against itself which can make you physically nervous. It's the blood sugar falling too low that causes the jittery feeling, so they say. Most players are just the opposite; they eat way ahead of matches, preferring to play on an empty stomach. Metabolisms differ greatly. Mine must be specially fast, particularly when I'm a little nervous and go through any amount of food in a hurry.

My eating habits would actually meet the approval of the strictest nutritionist without even trying. Luckily, I love to eat all the foods that are supposed to be good for one; meats, proteins, vegetables and fruit. In fact, I hate eating junk food. The reason for this is, I suppose, a strict dietary upbringing. White sugar was unavailable in the house, soft drinks had no chance of getting into the refrigerator and white bread was absolutely forbidden. I remember at about five years old in Cape Town, Judy and I used to go over to our neighbours on the pretext of playing games. What we really went for was the white bread and jam that was offered.

My mother is just as intractable about food now. She grows all her own vegetables, abhorring artificial fertilisers, and makes her own whole wheat bread out of organically grown wheat. Her favourite reading matter is published by the Soil Association.

If Fred, the gardener, suggests tackling the clover and daisies on the tennis lawn with weed-killer, she nearly has a fit.

Together, with the help of a giant steaming compost heap, they create a masterpiece of a vegetable garden that could change the mind of any non-vegetable loving child.

I stabbed my fork into some ham and limp lettuce hoping not really to spear any successfully. I eyed the plate and was met by the reproachful stare of an insipid hard-boiled egg. My sizeable appetite had shrunk to the proportions of a Lenten fast. The food peristalted down my throat in practically unchewed lumps.

It was comparatively quiet everywhere. The throng of people that usually populated the area below was absent. Most of the ticket-holders hadn't arrived yet for the finals; the standing-roomers were doing their best to get positioned, and there was a huge mob queuing up at the other end to catch a glimpse of the Queen as she arrived at the grounds.

I pushed my plate aside. I made a feeble attempt to eat some bread and then a little ice cream. You're supposed to eat carbohydrates before strenuous exercise. Protein takes too long to digest.

The clock on the wall hardly seemed to move. I didn't know how I was going to spend another one and a half hours. "What if I run away? What if I just decide to disappear without telling anyone? I would cause quite a stir!" It was one of those vertiginous fantasies like thinking when you're in a moving car "What would happen if I opened the door and jumped out?"

The waitress snapped me out of my motiveless caprice. "Are you finished with this, can I take away your plate?" I nodded yes and looked out of the window again. There was a lone figure in the stands of the Number Two court looking at me; not staring, just looking. I recognised her. It was the schoolgirl who'd made me a hand-crafted "Good Luck" card at the beginning of the week. I'd given her a ticket into the ground one day and she told me she had an exam on the afternoon of the final.

I wondered how she'd evaded it. I waved her over. From under the window she told me she managed to write her exam in the morning and was going to stand and watch the score tick off on the big scoreboard on the mall. I recalled my own days as a frustrated spectator, so I scribbled a note on a napkin from the table requesting the commissionaire at the competitors' stand to squeeze her in. The seats aren't numbered; I was sure she could fit in on the stairs if necessary. When I sat in the members' stand before the match I saw her in the front row. I was happy he'd let her in and that she had a good seat.

I walked out to play, feeling a distant rumbling in my stomach. I balanced myself to serve at 1–0. I was moving fast, pumping myself. It wasn't because I needed more adrenalin; I wanted to avoid dreaming. It wasn't an unconscious rush though, I was taking my time when it mattered, pacing around in circles. I knew why I was moving fast. I wanted to keep occupied.

Betty was composed in comparison, even subdued. I

wondered whether she was a little tired. It must have seemed to her like a lions' den. I knew how, in Rome, when a foreigner played an Italian on the Campo Centrale, the hapless competitor was compared to a Christian being thrown to the lions in the Colosseum. Actually, to enter that Centre Court one comes out through a sort of underground passage which does something to perpetuate the impression. Maybe when we walked out to play this afternoon Betty had had visions of a pack of unicorns waiting for her.

For sixteen years I had been one of Wimbledon's ninety-six satellites orbiting with a chance every 365 days to land on that consecrated ground. Every year I had miscalculated my opportunity for a successful mission and hurtled further away. If I didn't make it soon, I was doomed to orbit eternally.

As I won my serve for 2–0 I felt my mass assume its weight for the first time. I had passed the line of demarcation into Wimbledon's magnetic field, and was being drawn irreversibly toward my destiny.

I waited to return serve; on my toes, twisting my racquet handle around, gritting my teeth. My bottom lip was beginning to hurt from biting it.

I attacked the serve. Betty rushed a little and hit an infirm volley. She must have been getting flustered. I won the next point. Two more points and I'd have another break. My return missed by inches. She heaved a sigh of relief but her involvement was receding into the background. She was showing signs of resignation.

She levelled at 30–30, almost accidentally hitting an

153

untakable shot. When she hit a volley out to give me 40–30, the crowd were nearly unruly. As they visualised the moment of victory, every point I won became a minor celebration in preparation for the big one.

"Please try to keep quiet," the umpire requested. After a brief moment they collected themselves.

We were back in action.

My six weeks of intense training during Team Tennis were paying off. I'd never been fitter. It's the greatest feeling psychologically to know your stamina won't give out and that not many balls can get past you.

Tennis is the best training for tennis. The greatest asset in playing Team Tennis, I find, is the constant availability of practice courts and partners. With the New York Apples, I play as much with Sandy Mayer, Ray Ruffels and Fred Stolle as I do with the girls. No one babies you around. As Fred says, if you complain when he whacks a ball straight at you at the net, "Give you another fifty of those and you'll make damn sure you get out of the way and hit them!" In the end you develop such a pride in your ability to keep up that you'd rather die than admit you can't breathe, your legs are aching and your heart is about to burst right out of your chest.

I raced from one side of the court to the other, chasing what were probable winners, but knowing that if I could scrape them back Betty would be forced to make the shot. It's demoralising if your opponent never gives up.

154

Deuce on Betty's serve.

I stretched for a backhand return. The ball left my racquet with a purr. It was one of those shots. The second I touched it I knew it was good.

The next point I won on a double fault.

That double was literally the point that won the match; it gave me two breaks of serve.

The atmosphere was reminiscent of Christmas Day when the guests have all just arrived. The preliminaries to the presentation of the turkey are starting. Everyone joins in making the last-minute adjustments to the table, putting the presents under the tree, adding wood to the fire in the hearth. The bottle of champagne is the cynosure of all eyes as it's deftly opened by cautious fingers. The aroma of the turkey mingles with the scent of the burning wood reminding them that there's very little time left to wait.

On the Centre Court the 15,000 guests sat savouring the festivities to come.

"Miss Wade leads by three games to love in the final set."

We changed ends and I sat with my towel on my lap. It reminded me of Ceddy, the black cat at Queen's who'd sat on my lap earlier that morning. He was my good-luck charm for the tournament.

Black cats have always been the only real super-
stitious omen I believe in. It doesn't matter if they
cross the road from the left to right or vice versa, as
long as they select me to run in front of.

Once I was about to play Margaret Court in the
final of the Dewar Cup. I felt rather cheerless about
the encounter as I'd lost several times in a row to her.
I badly wanted to win this, my last chance of the
series.

As I drove home late that semifinal night after the
tennis, wondering what I could do to create that
ounce more self-confidence, a black cat raced across
the street in front of my car causing me to brake
suddenly. I glanced at my watch; it was the stroke of
midnight and immediately I knew I would win the
match. The next day I played as if I'd always beaten
Margaret and won in two comfortable sets.

Ceddy was the most beautiful, friendly cat. Each
morning I'd practised at Queen's during the tournament he'd be there sitting in the sun or under a hedge
or inside the lounge ready to talk and purr.

I'd been wooing all the black cats in London; Lucky
I, Lucky II, Blackie, Sootie, the lot. Have you ever
noticed how many handsome arrogant black cats
there are in London? But Ceddy was my personal
guardian against bad luck.

That morning, he'd been there as usual waiting to
be admired and cosseted, turning his best side to the
cameras that were trying to take candid pictures of

me. Generally, photographers drive me crazy when I'm looking for some peace to concentrate, but with Ceddy in my arms I didn't mind.

He was probably stretched out on the grass right now, oblivious of his role this afternoon.

The crowd lifted me as I walked out to the Royal Box end. It was my serve to come. I just kept moving, driving myself, exhorting myself. I had never been so eager in my life.

Each point I won was like adding dry hay to a burning barn. If Betty won a point it was as effective at dampening the crowd's enthusiasm as a pail of water would be on the crackling bales.

I hit a couple of good volleys; she missed a few shots. It was my seventh straight game. At 30–30 I'd hit a backhand volley deep down the line, which she reached and made a smooth, tough forehand back down my line. I dived for it and converted what she must have thought was a certain winner into my own winning shot. There was disbelief all over Betty's face.

The sensation of hitting that shot reminded me of some of the flashy winners that flowed coolly off the

racquet of Maria Bueno at her best. When I was a teen-
ager I used to watch every match of hers to absorb the
rhythm and timing of her strokes so that I might
endeavour to reproduce them.

On the Monday Wimbledon started, as had
happened many years previously, I'd been amongst a
group of players gathered around the television set at
Queen's Club, wanting to be part of the moment the
championships opened. This year it was something
more. As part of a ceremony to celebrate the
centenary of the club, all the past champions paraded
in a splurge of sentiment to the strains of "Auld Lang
Syne".

The title "Wimbledon champion" always bears such
an aura of respect and emotion. Here were fifty past
champions; some I'd only heard about, some I'd
watched perform. Some I liked, some I didn't; some
much younger than I, some old enough to be my
grandparents. They were the élite, the few people
who had succeeded in winning the most sought-after
laurel in the tennis world.

I left the television to go outside to practise. There
was Maria pulling up in a cab. Surprised to see her
here so soon I said, "Gee, Maria, I just saw you a few
minutes ago on the television. You looked great. I
wish I could have been there." She smiled, almost as
if she had a pretty good idea what would happen in
the next two weeks. "Don't worry," she said, "you
will."

Today before my match again she said, "Virginia, you'll win. You're playing so much better than all the others. You have to win."

Arthur Ashe had also sent me a good-luck note that day. Arthur and I share the same birthday (he's two years older) and our luck has run much the same course. We both won the US Open the same year. He won Wimbledon when he was thirty-one and now I was thirty-one. We regarded each other's fortunes with an interested eye.

Betty served, beginning to look a little numbed by the whole thing. I chipped the serve back, she hit a forehand wide back to where I'd come from. I turned on the spot and lunged at my forehand for a winner. The next point I hit a lob over her head that brought up chalk. 0–30.

She served wide to my forehand. I stretched and swung. The ball came from near the top of my racquet for a clean winner. 0–40.

The crowd were hardly watching the tennis any more, just putting up with the excruciating wait for the end.

Again the umpire asked for silence.

"OK," I thought, "don't worry if she hits a streak now . . . she always does when she's 0–40 . . . it can't last long

. . . if she wins a couple of points you've just got to be patient . . . don't imagine anything other than the score . . . the crowd is with you whatever happens."

Sure enough Betty played a series of magnificent shots. I scrambled, dived, retrieved, but Betty won her last game of the match.

Sitting down I forgot about those few irredeemable points. I'd win the next game on my serve then would be able to press for her serve and the match.

I was sure it would be the final change-over.

"This is the last time I'll be sitting in this chair for a whole year. My racquet cover's there . . . I'll put my racquet away first . . . you feel silly putting it away much later . . . my sweater . . . shall I put it on or not? . . . maybe I will . . . I like the colour . . . it's nice and soft too . . . I wonder whether Teddy's disappointed that I've worn this dress again . . . but I like it . . . I feel good in it . . . and it does have a perfect record . . ."

I had phoned Teddy Tinling about a month before Wimbledon to discuss my wardrobe for the tournament. During Team Tennis you get so used to wearing the same uniform night after night you tend to forget that all-white dresses are obligatory at Wimbledon.

Our Team Tennis dresses for 1977 were at least made by Teddy, so they were attractive and did fit well, but when you wear a dress that looks like an Italian flag cach night for six weeks the novelty pales.

I was thrilled to have five new ones, all in fresh white. There's nothing quite as therapeutic as a nice new dress to make you feel ready for the fray. Clothes do wonders for your ego, especially on the Centre Court.

Teddy Tinling designs, not just dresses, but creations. He doesn't merely cover you up; he gives you a sartorial extension of your personality. The result is something so clearly representative of each of his models that if ten dresses were hung up on a rack I bet you'd be able to pick out which player each one was for.

Between New York, London and Kent I must have close to two hundred dresses from the time when I was eighteen. I cannot bear to throw them out. Occasionally my sister or close friends get one passed down, but mostly they're hanging carefully covered up in a cupboard.

One of the latest Wimbledon dresses was embellished with handsome silver embroidery. In his charming, flattering way, Teddy said to me this year, "The silver dress is for you to wear on finals day so that you can say to the Queen, 'Ma'am, I had this specially designed in honour of your Jubilee.' "

Teddy knows more about women's tennis than

almost anybody. He recognises each girl's emotional state and his expert eye detects the addition of any excess ounces on physiques. Over the years he has been one of the constant friends on the tennis scene.

I banished any further reflections about my silver dress, hanging in the dressing room unused.

I walked out to serve. The crowd applauded from the minute we stood up all the way to the baseline.

"This is your last service game of the championships . . . take your time . . . make it good . . . you only need to win four points . . ."

15–0 . . .

"That's one . . ."

Again I served. It was a long rally. Betty miss-hit a high volley.

"That's two . . . another two for this game . . . I wonder how I'll react when I win . . . I weep whenever I watch other people . . . will I jump over the net? . . . will I throw my racquet in the air? . . . will I drop to my knees like Manuel Orantes after that emotional victory at Forest Hills . . . will I do something crazy like forgetting to shake hands . . ."

When I beat Chris I behaved normally until I sat down

*to collect my stuff and I saw a bank of photographers . . .
then I suddenly felt like weeping . . . This was the final.
That was only the semi, but that match meant so much."*

I'd looked forward to playing Chris in the semifinal.
During Eastbourne, where we were playing the week
before, the draw for Wimbledon had come out. It
looked fine to me. Every draw is much the same. If
you're going to win the tournament you have to beat
everyone. But, of course, the press immediately
issued headlines "Tough on Ginny", etc.

They all believed Chris was invincible. During the
tournament when I'd watched the BBC highlights in
the evenings I heard the commentator say so many
times, "I don't think anyone can successfully rival the
champion with the exception of perhaps Mrs King."
(Chris had made short shrift of Billie Jean in the
quarterfinal, 6–2 6–1.) My name wasn't even men-
tioned. I knew I could beat her. I wanted to. I also
wanted to prove myself finally to all those doubters.

In the dressing room there is always an atmosphere
of different shades of mood. One is very susceptible
to variations, but if you're feeling in control, you
manage to observe the undercurrents of nerves and
confidence without being affected. In previous years I
have found it to be one of the hardest elements of the

tournament to contend with. It seemed so difficult to retain a fragile equanimity when everyone around me was in a similarly brittle state.

This year I was so composed that I never felt my identity diminish for a minute. The latent fears in the other players were perceptible. I felt stronger than anyone.

My quarterfinal match against Rosie Casals might have been something to worry about as I'd lost to her several times on the Virginia Slims circuit in the previous months. I'd been in a transitional stage and I was fighting the temptation to return to my old habitual service in moments of threat. This week I'd been completely comfortable with my service and the determination to be in the finals got me through a spot of trouble in the match against her.

I had overcome that and was through to my allocated seeding spot against Chris.

It was just what I wanted; to play on the Centre Court at Wimbledon the opponent whom everyone categorically considered the No 1 woman player in the world. It was a perfect *mise-en-scène*.

I knew what I wanted to do against Chris and she knew I could beat her. I had rehearsed sufficiently to trust myself fully during the performance. My training was there, and I was calm and collected throughout the entire time.

I lost the middle set, but that didn't deflect my main objective to get to the finals. In the third set I felt stronger as each point passed and captured it losing only one game.

Almost before the win had registered I shook hands with Chris, who congratulated me in her usual way, epitomising good sportsmanship.

When I sat down, very tired and happy, and looked up to see the cameras on me, it struck home that I'd won the match. Now I could keep my promise to win the finals.

I had to force myself to think of something else, not to be overcome with tears at the relief of having actually achieved what I'd put so much effort and emotion into.

By the time I reached the dressing room, a few minutes later, the exhilaration had well and truly sunk in. There on the television were the commentators still uttering confounded words of amazement. I delightedly thrust my fist at the screen, to the hilarity of the few players in the room.

Today I had no axes to grind. They all expected me to win. But matches have to be won with total commitment and

effort, whoever is on the other side of the net. Just because I had a good record against Betty it didn't mean I could relax. She's much too tough a competitor. She'd also already beaten Martina Navratilova and Sue Barker en route to the final.

I carried on with my service game. There was a comparative hush as we played each point out, followed by precipitate applause as I won one more point, then another.

I was 5–1 up.

I needed only one more game, only four more points.

Betty took the new balls to serve. She served way out to my right. The ball seemed to have passed me, but I swooped out at it. I just got my racquet on it. It skimmed through the air. Betty thought she'd aced me and when it landed on her side she wasn't there. She shook her head incredulously.

The points rolled past as the velocity on the unalterable course increased. There were voices shouting above the applause now, screams as I reached 15–40.

Two match-points to me.

I raced to the ball; it was too good. I even slipped in my effort.

Second match-point.

Betty served wide to my backhand in the left court. It skipped off the tape and into the tram-line. Fault.

She tossed up the ball for her last serve. I moved around to take it on my forehand; I went down the line at her feet. She bent for the forehand volley. It was too low; too wide. The return was perfect.

There was a tumultuous explosion. I sprinted to shake

hands. What could I say but "Thanks" to Betty. She patted my head; she graciously offered congratulations.

Everything was happening so fast around me.

I thanked the umpire.

The blond ballboy asked for my sweat-band as his souvenir.

The photographers swarmed around my chair.

I zipped my racquet in its cover and grabbed my sweater.

I took my brush out of my handbag and brushed my hair.

I was being swept along with the same momentum as the crowd, with the same crashing sound in my ears.

I could almost watch myself from the outside, smiling at the battery of cameras as I wiped my damp hands on my towel.

Now I seemed to have time on my hands to hear the whistling, yelling, clapping. The noise as the umpire began to make an announcement. "Ladies and Gentlemen," I listened wondering what he was going to say. "The score was 4–6, 6–3, 6–1." Another burst of cheering and laughter went up.

I grinned. "That was me! I won! I won Wimbledon!"

I was overcome with a shining joy. It wasn't that I'd done something great and was feeling the exhaustion or relief of a Titanic effort. It was simply the surge of elation coursing through me.

I wanted to jump up and down.

I wanted to embrace everybody in the stadium.

It wasn't a complex emotion. It was pure.

It was just joy.

I looked around me. The people were all standing. It looked like the last night of the Proms, with the Union Jacks waving their own congratulations.

The red carpet was rolled out . . . Near it stood the flag-bedecked table.

The Queen was leaving the Royal Box.

The Duchess of Kent was on her feet clapping . . . I waved at her. She raised her arms aloft and shook her fists in a gesture of victory.

It all sped by: a montage of every sight I'd ever wanted.

Like an actor frozen backstage I felt the hand of the stage manager shoving me towards Her Majesty. I curtsied and shook hands.

The plate was in my grasp.

I watched the Queen's mouth moving. I knew she was talking to me, but with all the noise I didn't have much idea what she was saying.

The next thing I remember was Betty encouraging me to hold the salver higher. It had been a tough afternoon for her. There was every reason for her to feel excluded, but she joined in with the gallantry of a great sport.

The voices yelling, "Over here, Virginia!" were drowned by probably the first chorus of "For She's a Jolly Good Fellow" that's ever been raised on the Wimbledon Centre Court.

I felt completely familiar with everyone; I knew each one of these people and they knew me. We were like a huge family rejoicing en masse.

Some action shots during Wimbledon 1977

Surrounded by cameramen after the Final

Moment of triumph, with the Queen and the Duke of Kent looking on.
On the far left is Mr David Mills, Secretary of the All England Club and
behind him, Sir Carl Aarvold, President of the Lawn Tennis Association

At Sharsted with the family, (*left to right*): **Father, Mother, Auntie Phyllis and Auntie Daw**

With a very happy Mother

Bjorn Borg and Virginia toasting each other after their respective wins at the All England Lawn Tennis Club's Champions' Dinner

Pictured here with Geoffrey Boycott at the *Daily Express* Sportsman and Sportswoman of the Year presentations

We had been through a whole life together. We had tried and tried. Finally we'd all made the dream happen.

On the hundredth birthday of Wimbledon; in the year of the Queen's Jubilee, I once again raised the victory plate and silently thanked everyone for this exquisite moment; for believing in me, for caring and for waiting.

Current events become history; they're supplanted by new experiences that absorb one's attention. They belong in the past, but they exist perpetually by colouring everything from that point on. People continually ask me how winning Wimbledon has changed my life. Have I come down from "cloud nine"? Has there been a let-down?

I never *was* on cloud nine. My happiness was conscious; from the deep satisfaction of achieving what I had set out to do. The reward for that is permanent. It didn't change me. The changes occurred before; winning was a ramification of that. It has just imbued my life with a richer tone. It has created a feeling of potency that one can convert situations and environment into assets not liabilities. You don't have to be manipulated into an habitual pattern by circumstances.

How often does one hear people in a general sort of malaise swearing that if their career would pick up, so would their happiness? Career and personal life are closely interlinked. It is almost impossible for one not to influence the other. To think that the former dictates the latter, however, is putting the cart before the horse.

First, my thinking altered off the court. I developed a stronger sense of self; this stayed with me wherever I went. My tennis reflected it. This visible result showed me that the effort was worthwhile. The wins that used to leave me with a feeling of emptiness because they were independent of inner security, now are like guiding posts to assure me I'm on the right track. They are a manifestation of my personal progress. They occur when I've worked hard enough and when I want to win enough.

There's an intellectual satisfaction in assessing the challenge and effecting the solution. Now I know that, if I'm prepared to put in that effort again, there is the basis and potential to attain what I want.

Because I had to work to find the means to win Wimbledon, it has a greater depth of import for me. If it had come ten years ago it might have abridged the maturity I've been obliged to develop.

I never doubted I'd win someday. If I didn't want it enough earlier, I sensed I would later and could meet the demands. Having taken so long is immaterial; it matters only that I finally did do it.

Tennis is like a game of chess, with limitless different approaches. You can never reach perfection, but you can always strive for it. When you've improved one thing there is another to work on.

Matches are an encapsulated version of any expression in life: they are confrontations with people and circumstance. There are goals to meet; obstacles to override; choices and decisions to be made under pressure. There are personal selfish moods to be submerged; strategies to be mapped and likewise changed if they don't work. You have to know who you are; what you're realistically capable of and what you want out of a situation. Then you have to be disciplined to follow the way you know is idealistically right, even if it may be rougher to pass.

Whether you're a tennis player, housewife, salesman, teacher, executive or whatever, when you're professional at living, you're professional at whatever you do. You can reap the reward of knowing where you stand at each juncture. Tennis, for me, has produced even more, through the external acknowledgment of my efforts.

In fact, if you ever want anybody to notice you, just win Wimbledon.

I never realised so many people could watch a tennis match in so many countries. Letters were sent from all over the world; Canada, America, Australia, South Africa, India, Pakistan, Japan, Malta, Europe, not to mention all those from home. Such reaction was a stunning hymn to the principle of abiding by one's convictions. Having all that attention was very humbling. Each time I've been saluted since then, I've felt the same way. I enjoy the praise mainly because it seems to elevate the spirits of the donors. It provides an instant of communication, knowing I've contributed to someone's happiness.

From the aspect of fame, the adulation means comparatively little. I know it is transient and that public memory is short. While it lasts I'll enjoy it, but when it's over I won't be disappointed.

As we turned the corner behind the wall of the Centre Court I broke into a run for the dressing room where I knew my family and a few close friends would be. I got three steps before being intercepted first by NBC television then another three steps to where the press go-between ushered me into the subterranean interview room bulging with reporters.

Hours later I arrived up there only to be begged by importunate photographers for more pictures outside with the plate. Together with the family we went to the balcony high above the ground. Beneath us what started off as a scattering of people mushroomed into a throng, hurraying each time I held the trophy up for the cameras. The cheering all over again was like an encore to the fiesta on court.

They stayed till the films were expended and I was released to go to change. At the bottom of the stairs a pair of hands reached out to me and a searching voice asked, "Ginny, is it really true? Please tell me it's true!" It was a blind girl called Mary, whom I'd been aware of for years as one of my most ardent supporters. She clasped me to her and for the first time all afternoon tears welled up in my eyes.

Eventually, in the midst of the retinue, I left the grounds, past the applauding spectators already waiting on line for the men's final, past the man peddling newspapers with my picture all over the front and headed with family and friends for the cars.

Near Sloane Square we saw a group outside a TV shop window intently watching dozens of screens with the replay of the match on. We pulled up and asked who'd won. They answered, then recognised me. Waving, we took off for our champagne.

Saturday raced by in a gentle blur of fatigue. First on the agenda of the day was a visit to the newspaper stand. For once I could indulge myself by buying every paper, indeed several copies of some.

For the last time that year, I went out to Wimbledon, glad to be an authentic spectator and

173

delight in every moment of artistic contest in the men's finals.

Then there was tea with the Duke and Duchess of Kent. In between niceties with the King and Queen of Greece, the Archbishop of Canterbury, George Solti and other such luminaries, I managed to procure enough cucumber sandwiches to appease my athlete's appetite.

When I expressed my appreciation for the enthusiasm of HRH the Duchess after the match, she laughingly told me, "I got into trouble with my daughter. She phoned me from school and said, 'Mother, what *were* you doing? My friends at school thought it was a trifle unseemly.' I said to her, 'But it was Ginny, we know her!' "

Their being so effusive in their congratulations had meant so much to me.

I heard later that André Previn had been rehearsing with the LSO during the match. They were interrupted by a messenger, who handed a note to the conductor. He stopped the rehearsal to announce, "Our Ginny has won," and apparently everyone stood up and applauded.

The Sunday was brilliant with sunshine. Sharsted saw us decked out in shorts, sprawling on the velvet grass. All my friends played tennis; I ballgirled and periodically substituted for a player taking "time-out".

The press somehow infiltrated. I didn't feel like

resisting anyone so I obliged by stretching out on a garden chair, an empty bottle of champagne on the ground.

Lunch was an Epicurean delight with garden vegetables and strawberries and cream. The conversation inevitably ended up revolving around me. Daddy told how, when aged three, I'd brandished a hammer at his austere secretary. Mummy told how, if I'd invited punishment, I'd writhe and kick in her arms so that she couldn't do anything with me. Auntie Daw, my mother's sister, told how I'd hug and squeeze her till she'd have to beg to be let go. Judy, about mothering me when I was about five and worrying I'd hurt myself tearing all over. Christopher remembered how I always climbed the door jambs, spreadeagled and then yelled for everyone to look at me: the athletic little exhibitionist.

My other friends chuckled at all the family stories. And silently I'm sure each of us mourned that Anthony, so physically and temperamentally like me, was no longer with us.

Later, Mother showed me the gigantic lime tree. Apparently, at four hundred years, it was the oldest in Kent. On the dot of 1.00 p.m. on Friday, the day I won, it had split and come crashing down.

That was on July 1st. Everything happened to me in ones this year. In previous years I had tried to manipulate numbers to augur well for me, experimenting with sevens and fives; adding the digits on my Wimbledon competitor's badge; considering the numerals on hotel doors. Nothing ever happened that could connect good luck with numbers. Then in the month or so prior to Wimbledon there was a sudden abundance of ones.

On the first of June, I looked at the odometer of my car and every digit was a one. My brother's baby boy was born on the same day. When I got to Wimbledon my competitor's badge was 101. In the twenty-four hours before my final, random panic thoughts filtered through my mind. Suddenly on the Friday morning as I was still searching for the absolutely correct frame of mind, I realised it was July first. From that moment I was positive I'd win.

From the quintessential home of tennis I was swept by a jet to the space-age hybrid counterpart of the game—World Team Tennis. From the lawns of the All England Club and the regulation whites we went straight back to the multi-coloured carpet (red, brown, green and blue) and our garish uniforms.

The league consists of teams in New York (Apples), Boston (Boston Lobsters), Indiana (Indiana Loves),

Cleveland (Cleveland Nets), Los Angeles (Los Angeles Strings), San Francisco (San Francisco Gaters), San Diego (San Diego Friars), Phoenix (Phoenix Racquets), Seattle (Seaport Cascades) and the tenth which last year had no home base as it came from the Soviet Union.

Each team has a minimum of six players, three men and three women. Fifty per cent of the matches are played at home and the other half are away. The Soviet tennis players are still called amateurs, but there was an agreement reached between the league and Soviet Federation which resulted in the Russians playing in such an ultra-professional arrangement. Unfortunately for the players, who did all the work, the Federation received all the money.

The scoring system is entirely different. There are no 15s or 30s; love becomes zero; and at what should be deuce, three points all, the game is decided by the next point.

Even the officials don't operate in the conventional way. The umpire stands; the linesmen travel up and down the court covering more than one line. There are still bad calls but at least they don't get stiff and stagnant from being in sedentary positions. Actually, there is no line; just a seam between the various colours.

After a while the colours of the court don't surprise one at all. It is only people like Australian Phil Dent who is colour blind and those watching black-and-white television that have to play by memory or discern varying shades of grey.

During an evening five sets are played. One set each of men's and women's singles and doubles and one mixed. The score is accumulated over the evening and the close matches become contests of seismic consequence. Certainly, if the volume of noise, shouting, foot-stamping is any calibration, the outcome is of earth-shaking significance.

It isn't tennis for the connoisseur who appreciates the development of strategies and the emerging dominance of superiority. But it is full of action for those who prefer excitement to subtlety.

For a player it is different from normal matches, but it is just as challenging. While you're on court the remaining five team members sit on a bench at the side gesticulating and egging you on vocally. The team owner joins in with prompting and you feel nothing more pressing than to win as many games as you can and lose as few.

You develop a tremendous support for your team. In the general noise your manners do have a tendency to deteriorate as you can say almost anything and nobody hears you.

While you're on court it is all-absorbing. In between it is an impersonal life of aeroplanes, hotel rooms and unfamiliar faces. Even the members of the opposing teams enter your precincts for scarcely more than a hasty "Hello, how are you?" As a team you work and co-operate together; otherwise, it's all pretty much the same.

The only thing that separates one match from another is the clique of loyal home fans including one who sometimes brings in delicious home-made Italian food; lasagne, canneloni, ravioli and meatballs; manna in the wilderness of fast food. We have to stash it all in the whirlpool of the training room and lock the door to make sure Sandy Mayer doesn't eat everything before the other players have even clapped eyes on it. At one sitting Sandy's been known to consume a dozen hamburgers, three milkshakes, a quart of orange juice, two salads, plus a couple of ice-cream sundaes and a handful of candy bars.

Team Tennis forces you to learn to concentrate through whatever bedlam is going on about you. (Ilie Nastase sometimes rang a cowbell to put the other team off.) Once you've played in such circumstances you'll never again notice a baby crying in the stands or a person moving about.

Also the practice and drilling are more orderly and systematic than in the tournaments, with a bevy of ready partners and ample court time.

Practice isn't an excessive number of hours. It's the intensity with which you address yourself to it that's important. Your mind has to be alert as it is in a match, or else you get bored and before you know it you are hitting the shots sloppily. You have to keep devising methods of keeping your mind interested.

Something might work for a while, then it becomes second-hand and has to be replaced by a fresh idea.

There are two levels of consciousness; the main concentration on the job at hand and the secondary almost ethereal layer that flits around from one inconsequential thing like, "I need more petrol in the car," to another, "I'm in the mood for Japanese food."

Strangely, when your immersion is greatest you're more aware of the floaty thoughts. There's a delicate line when the nonsense takes over and your proper attention is interrupted. This is when you have to produce an artifice to realign your thinking.

Your muscles need to be warmed up too. There are constant new developments in theories of athletic training and diet. In the last few years stretching has become a must. It makes tremendous sense, not only warming up muscles properly and preventing injuries but improving flexibility as well.

Each player needs different requirements. My game has to have a high degree of flexibility and speed. Other types need more strength and stamina. There is a trend towards weight training. Lots of players are working with weights to develop lesser muscles and eliminate weaknesses. It's not so much to develop the brawn as to maximise motor operation. I haven't tried it yet, but I might.

After Wimbledon I was met in each city we played with standing ovations and receptions that overwhelmed me. I was busy the whole time with demands for interviews, but it didn't matter because I had something to talk about. I actually prefer being busy all the time, operating according to a schedule of things that have to be done. When they're complete it's not long before I start off again with appearances for a sports company, a photographic session for a motor car advertisement, a commercial for a headache tablet.

I'm the touring pro for a beautiful resort on Captiva Island in Florida called South Seas Plantation. I can practise amongst the palm trees or forget about tennis and collect shells on the beach. I can't escape there often enough, but to know there is somewhere within easy reach exuding peace, is a very comforting thought, especially when the tennis begins to hang heavily.

The season continued. We won the World Team Tennis play-offs beating the Phoenix Racquets in the finals, where I beat Chris Evert 6–0. It was our second consecutive year as Team Tennis champions.

I plunged directly into Forest Hills and I gained more renown by playing Renée Richards in the first round and commentating on television than for my results.

My tennis feats recovered the next week in Japan when I won a big tournament there. Tokyo is a long haul from New York, but the contrast between the two is a refreshing change.

I actually like living in New York. As a visitor staying in hotels and being faced with the hustle from morning till night I found it rather inhospitable. It seemed hostile and even more exhausting than any other large city. But having a base there I can find my way around. I know where to shop for different foods, where to eat well but casually and enjoy the multitude of activities. London is still my favourite city to live in, but in New York I can be a little more incognito and informal.

Tokyo is one of the few places where you look out of your hotel window and distinguish immediately that you're in another hemisphere. The hotels themselves tend to be western, but there are oriental flavours; a freshly laundered kimono on your bed each night, toothbrushes and mini tubes of paste in every bathroom, and a Japanese massage at any hour of the day.

The massage is hardly the gentle one that reaches nowhere near the origin of muscle tensions. You end up pleading with these little ladies as they seem to rip leg muscles apart and torture shoulders. Afterwards you feel terrific; whether from the relief that it's over, or because they really do succeed in relaxing the muscles, I'm not sure.

Over the few years I've been playing there I've become attached to the Japanese customs and formalities. We're mobbed by appreciative youngsters giggling with excitement, longing to receive autographs written in western writing.

I've made a few close friends and through them have gained an insight into the culture and have had a chance to negotiate areas the language barrier would otherwise prohibit.

I was delighted to win the tournament and to see my pictures all over the newspapers amidst the Japanese writing, and to be referred to as "Wade-san". For a few days I relaxed in the coutryside, away from the city, before heading back to the States and another event for television.

They've held this special tournament for several years down in Hilton Head, South Carolina. Four top men and four top women play singles, doubles and mixed, then accumulate points for the top place (male or female).

By the time we got to the mixed final, it was down to a close finish between Roscoe Tanner, Bjorn Borg and me. In fact, if I won with my partner Vitas Gerulaitis, I won the $50,000 first prize. If I lost, Roscoe won, Borg came in second and I third.

It was one of those mixed matches where everything combines to make each point a real drama. Roscoe's serve would leave me still waiting when it had ripped past me at 140 mph. Each time the crowd and I would laugh. Vitas played brilliantly. Kerry Reid and I were both good.

We had match points at 5–3 in the third set which slipped away. With mounting tension the score reached 6–6 and Kerry and Roscoe had two match points in the tie breaker. On one of them Kerry sent up a lob over my head. I thought about leaving it for Vitas, decided it was much too much on my side and thought, "There's no choice. I have to go for it." I reached up, just got the top of my racquet on it, thumped it and, thinking I'd missed it, started up for the net to shake hands. Vitas spun around. "It's in!! Great shot!" It had landed two inches from their baseline and neither hit it. They'd also expected it to go out.

A few points later we won and I got the first prize.

Since Colgate has come into the game as a major sponsor, the finale of the year is the Colgate

International Series Championships; the distaff side of the Colgate Masters, for the top eight players of the year and top four doubles pairs.

Frankie Durr and I won the doubles in October. I enjoy playing doubles, although singles receives preferential attention.

Over the years I've won all the major doubles titles (except Wimbledon) with Margaret Court: the US Open twice, the French Open, the Italian Open and the Bridgestone title. We combined well together. Her concentration was so steadfast that it brought mine up.

In 1975 we played King and Casals in the final of Forest Hills. The match was scheduled before the men's singles final and supposedly well in advance of the television coverage. It became a great match, overlapping, to the despair of the officials, into television time at about 4–3 in the third set. On literally the first point they picked up live, Margaret and I both ran for a lob, won the point but in the process got tangled up. Her engagement ring caught in the frills of my dress. We went on to win the match (unattached) which subsequently elicited a revival of interest in women's doubles.

Olga Morozova has been another of my favourite partners. She's very highly strung and I've always liked her sparkling personality, but sometimes I'd have to exert all my energies to keep that deep Russian emotion within the court. She doesn't dawdle round at the best of times, but when the situation gets tough I have to use my one Russian phrase, *"Teesha teesha, nyet te rapis"*—Slow down, don't rush—to keep her in check.

Kashmar (she approved my Russian nickname for her—it means nightmare) and I have become great friends. I regret so much that her national association places such strong limitations on her that she is unable to play most of the events.

I phoned her the night I won Wimbledon and she was so happy; only sorry she hadn't been there too. The year before she had come down to Kent with me and swopped Russian recipes with my mother. We missed her down there this time.

Now I'm such good friends with Olga, I would love to make a return visit to the Soviet Union, knowing more through an insider's experience. When I went to Russia about ten years ago, I had to rely on the judgment of interpreters. We communicated only sketchily with the other Soviet players, and they would constantly become totally ignorant of the English language when an awkward question was asked.

The people in general were enormously kind and generous, presenting you with gifts of all sorts, books, caviare, Russian dolls etc. Western clothes were in high demand, but you could never give them away, you had to sell them.

The joke was that the roubles you collected were of

no use whatsoever. There was absolutely nothing worth buying except with foreign currency. Even with that, the thing that I would have liked most, some decent food, was unobtainable.

I'm sure things have changed somewhat. Today, jeans are supposedly the most sought-after western commodity, replacing sweaters and stockings. But the portraits of Lenin that decorated every street corner must still be there. At least now, knowing Olga, I'd be assured of a decent meal.

Olga and I won the Italian championships, reached the final of Forest Hills and Bridgestone, the semifinal of Wimbledon and won several Virginia Slims tournaments.

Now I've resumed a partnership with Françoise Durr. Frankie's one of the best doubles players in the world. Playing with her is like being on a Saturday morning children's show. I love to watch her hitting crazy winners with her mongrel set of strokes. For a low backhand, her bottom nearly touches the ground. When I serve I always get the biggest kick out of watching her protract the acutest angles with her frying pan grip.

If things go wrong too often she reverts to swearing with such a strong Gallic accent that it is barely understandable. "Noooo . . . You idyot . . . watch za bawll!" as she clouts the top of her head with her racquet. Then she sees me laughing and her fury evaporates into a seraphic smile.

It's always worth watching her singles. You can be sure there'll be a jewel of a moment. Like the time in Monte Carlo when she was playing Helga Niessen, notorious for her leisurely change-overs. Helga had taken over the one solitary chair at the side of the court for her personal use, as her place to recover and aggravatingly sip the hot tea she'd brought in a thermos flask. Frankie had been winning and gradually her sizeable lead was whittled away. Her irritation was becoming obvious. Almost before she lost the point to be 6–5 down she raced from the baseline to this single chair and sat down with a wallop, crossing her arms and legs in a very definite statement of how she felt. Helga, showing no signs of being non-plussed, proceeded to stand by the umpire's chair and drink her tea, impervious to Frankie's glares.

After the Colgate championships, 1977 was rounded off from a tennis point of view by one final tournament in London; just in time for all the pre-Christmas parties. I was voted sportsperson of the year in every presentation that was made; the *Daily Express,* the Tennis Writers, the Sportswriters' Association and the BBC.

It seemed as if Wimbledon had only happened the day before and yet it gave me the feeling of being recognised as myself, not just as Virginia Wade the tennis player.

The essence of this and something I'll never quite

get over, was being the subject of "This is Your Life". Even as Eamonn Andrews with his red book filtered into my unsuspecting line of vision, it never entered my mind that there would actually be a show that night. I started to leave to get into tennis clothes for my scheduled practice session and refused to go. Then as the meaning of the event dawned on me and as every single person seemed to be in on it (except me) I changed my attitude. How they ever kept me from discovering it I'll never know. It was the best-kept secret since Jack Benny's age.

I was more nervous about the programme than I've ever been for any tennis match and then I proceeded to weep through the entire show.

All my family filed on. I thought Christopher was in Sweden where he lives. Then Auntie Gertie and Uncle Jim Filmer appeared from Queenstown, South Africa. We used to spend all our Christmas holidays on their farm there, and I'd seen them only once on one of my tennis trips to South Africa. Next on was Norman Brinker (Maureen Connolly's husband) and their daughter Cindy, my headmistress from Tunbridge Wells, then Frankie Durr and on and on. My eyes got bigger and bigger with surprise and tears of emotion. The others were all rehearsed and reacted as if television were their daily profession.

The tennis was over. 1977 was nearly over.

189

Winning Wimbledon is not only an accomplishment for me in terms of individual success; it exemplifies a principle I've always felt to be almost palpable.

Regardless of setting or obvious available means, one has the right, which need never be surrendered, to graduate, to ascend.

Within whatever context one exists, to focus on a realistic ambition and use every possible source of inspiration to confront the issues that separate you from what you want, is the spiritual inheritance of each of us.

As I watched the competitors during my first Wimbledon, it was with an emotion of mingled reverence and wonder. They were heroes ordained by some supernatural force. I worshipped them; a firm believer in their religion of superiority.

Until being one of them appeared to me a purpose I should verily pursue, I remained estranged from what I reasonably could have.

Once I became orientated to this end, the direction was automatically revealed.

The answers to each individual's pursuit was always there. One need only ask the right questions.

And the bottomless well of encouragment, when the motivation seems obscure or the result impossible, is there in every person who has ever planned and succeeded.

For me, seeing Wimbledon happen this year would be a constant reminder that what one truly wants is always possible.

It would always be there for me, and if I can personify that reminder for anyone else at any time, if only for a moment, our lives will continue on together permanently linked by the day I won Wimbledon . . .

DECEMBER 1977

Some of the Major Championship Titles won by Virginia Wade

Singles:

Rothmans British Hard Court Champion 1967, 1968, 1973, 1974
United States Open Champion 1968
Green Shield Welsh Open Champion 1971
Italian Champion 1971
Australian Champion 1972
Argentinian Champion 1972
Dewar Cup Champion 1969, 1973, 1974, 1975, 1976
Wimbledon Champion 1977

Doubles:

Benson & Hedges British Hard Court Champion 1967 with Ann Jones
Italian Champion with Margaret Court 1968
Italian Champion with Helga Mastoff 1971
Irish Open Champion with Margaret Court 1973
French Champion with Margaret Court 1973
United States Open Champion with Margaret Court 1973
Australian Champion with Margaret Court 1973
Italian Champion with Olga Morozova 1973
Benson & Hedges British Hard Court Champion 1974 with Julie Heldman
United States Open Champion with Margaret Court 1975
Bridgestone Champion with Margaret Court 1975